Dancing on the Rim of the World

VOLUME 19

SUN TRACKS

An American Indian Literary Series

Dancing on the Rim of the World

AN ANTHOLOGY OF CONTEMPORARY NORTHWEST NATIVE AMERICAN WRITING

Edited by ANDREA LERNER

Sun Tracks and The University of Arizona Press Tucson

The University of Arizona Press

Set in Linotron 202 Pilgrim.
∞ This book is printed on acid-free, archival-quality paper.
Manufactured in the United States of America.
94 93 92 91 90 5 4 3 2 1

LIBRARY OF CONGRESS CATALOGING IN PUBLICATION DATA

Dancing on the rim of the world : an anthology of contemporary Northwest Native American writing / edited by Andrea Lerner.
p. cm. — (Sun tracks ; v. 19)
Includes bibliographical references.
ISBN 0-8165-1097-0 (alk. paper). — ISBN 0-8165-1215-9 (pbk. : alk. paper)
1. American literature—Indian authors. 2. Indians of North America—Northwest, Pacific—Literary collections. 3. American literature—Northwest, Pacific. 4. American literature—20th century. I. Lerner, Andrea, 1954– II. Series.
PS501.S85 vol. 19
[PS508.I5]
810.8 s—dc20
[810.8′0897]
90-11006
CIP

British Library Cataloguing in Publication data are available.

For my mother, Marion Bresnick, who gave me a love for language and a language for love.

Contents

Acknowledgments xiii
Preface xv
The Rim of the World
An Introduction by Elizabeth Woody and Gloria Bird 1
JIM BARNES
One for Grand Ronde, Oregon 11
At the Burn on the Oregon Coast 12
Near Crater Lake 12
Contemporary Native American Poetry 13
GLORIA BIRD
Bare Bone Winter 17
Nine Months Waiting 17
GLADYS CARDIFF
Enoch Speaks of Omens 21
Pretty Bird 23
VICTOR CHARLO
Flathead River Creation 27
Dixon Direction 27
Frog Creek Circle 28
The Milltown 28
CHRYSTOS
I Have Not Signed a Treaty with the United States Government 33
Meditation for Gloria Anzaldua 34
Dear Mr. President 35
Winter Evening 36
Out the Top I Go 36
In the Grief River 37
JO WHITEHORSE COCHRAN
Halfbreed Girl in the City School 41

First of February, New Snow 42
Lover's Note 43
From My Grandmother 43
Nearing Winter 44

ROBERT DAVIS
Soulcatcher 47
Leveling Grave Island 48
Into the Forest 49
Danger Point, Bainbridge Island 49
Drowning 51

DEBRA CECILLE EARLING
Winter Keeps 55
Summer Humming 1946 56
Montana Burial Wind 57
Summer of Bees 60

ANITA ENDREZZE
The Dieter's Daughter 65
I Was Born 66
The Light That Passes 67
October Morning Walk 68
The Map-Maker's Daughter 69

MAXINE FRANKLIN
Skagit River Spirits 73
"Fields roll away . . ." 73
The Man Who Shot Ravens: Three Views 74
Wyoming Remembered 76

PHIL GEORGE
An-Himh Hi-hi (White Winter) 79
Grand Entry 79
Northwest Natives: Where Have All Our People Gone? 80
Thumbing Guy 82
Ice Fishin' 83

JANET CAMPBELL HALE
Ancestress 87
Autobiography in Fiction 88

ROGER JACK
An Indian Story 101
KING KUKA
For the Old Men Then and Now 115
All Medicine 116
Untitled 117
JUNE MCGLASHAN
Night After the Storm 121
Ever Have One of Those Days? 121
The Wait 122
Afraid 123
Devil's Night 123
A True Story 124
Seagull Egg Story 125
DIAN MILLION
The Highway 129
Currency 132
Invocation 133
Bainbridge: she thinks of home 135
NANCY NEAL
Julie-Anna 139
Christmas Poem 140
DUANE NIATUM
Round Dance 143
Son, This Is What I Can Tell You 143
Yellow Pine Cliff Song 145
Old Tillicum 146
NILA NORTHSUN
what the anthros don't hear 151
sometimes 152
hunter 153
hanblechia 154
two worlds 155
SANDRA OSAWA
The Makahs 159

My Song 160
The Catch 160
To Igogaruk 161
Two Brothers 162
AGNES PRATT
Empathy 165
So Quickly Came the Summer 165
Death Takes Only a Minute 166
Summer '76 166
May 1977 166
Reverie 167
RALPH SALISBURY
To Take Life, To Kill 171
VICKIE SEARS
The Orphanage Lost 181
Music Lady 183
GLEN SIMPSON
Front Street 189
Yukon River 189
Stick Dance, Nulato 190
Overnight at Boundary House, 1984 190
Steamers on the Yukon, 1944 191
The Shaman's Words 191
R. A. SWANSON
An Old Man Asks 195
Two Sisters 195
The Drums Touch 196
We Are All Warriors 197
The Wanderer's Prayer 197
"When the spirit moves you . . ." 198
MARY TALLMOUNTAIN
Untitled Poem 201
Koyukons Heading Home 203
Gaal Comes Upriver 204
The Spy's Nest 205

EARLE THOMPSON
Vigil 209
Design in Blue 209
She Walks in New-Born Leaves 210
Afternoon Vigil 211
Spirit 211
Whale Song 212
Dancer 213
GAIL TREMBLAY
Coyote, Hanging in a Museum, Comes Off the Wall 217
The Returning 218
It Is Important 219
Light Shakes 220
VINCE WANNASSAY
Murder on the Tri-Met 223
Observations 223
Broken Tradition 223
Treaties 224
Higher Power 225
JAMES WELCH
Riding the Earthboy 40 229
Christmas Comes to Moccasin Flat 229
The Only Bar in Dixon 230
Thanksgiving at Snake Butte 231
DAVID WHITED
Damn Moon; She's a Hard One! 235
Blending Wind & Stones 235
Empty Rats in the Cupboard 237
"The Modoc kind of remind me of the Nez Perce . . ." 237
RAMONA WILSON
Passing Battlefields 241
Spokane Museum 242
December on the Coast 242
Second Goodbye for Sue 243

ELIZABETH WOODY
In Memory of Crossing the Columbia 247
Hand into Stone 247
Of Steps to Drowning 248
Originating Fire 249
WILLIAM S. YELLOW ROBE, JR.
The Burning of Uncle 253
Bibliography 261
Publication and Portrait Credits 265

Acknowledgments

This project was completed with the assistance of grants from the following organizations: the Oregon State University Research Council, the Oregon Committee for the Humanities, the Oregon Arts Council, and the National Endowment for the Humanities.

There are a great many individuals who assisted me with the project, far too many to name here. But in particular, at Oregon State University, I would like to say a special thank you to my research assistants Barbara Nehler and Matthew Thiessen who did much of my homework for me, and to my colleague Simon Johnson whose advice and humor saw the project through from the beginning. Throughout the project a number of writers and scholars shared ideas and gave support. In particular, I wish to thank Joseph Bruchac, Phil Foss of the Institute of American Indian Arts, Jan Steinbright of the Institute of Alaska Native Arts, and from the beginning and through every stage, Barry Lopez. I would also like to thank all of the participants of the 1988 NEH Summer Seminar in Tucson, Arizona, on the Oral Tradition in Native American Literature, as well as Larry Evers, the director, for their insights and encouragement. And I wish to thank Gene Warneke for his patience and affection, and my dog, Shoshone, for taking me for walks in lovely places. I am indebted.

I also offer thanks to my editor, Greg McNamee, for his steadfast commitment to the project as well as his wise counsel, humor, and his friendship. Also at the University of Arizona Press, I wish to thank Patricia Shelton, my copy editor, for her discerning and scrupulous attention to the manuscript, as well as her gifts of affection.

Finally, I would like to thank the Northwest Native American communities for their generosity and assistance. And most importantly, I am indebted to the writers themselves, who gave not only their work, but their time, energy, and friendship. It has been a blessing.

ANDREA LERNER

Preface

Winters in western Oregon tend to be wonderful times for catching up on reading, for starting new projects, or for sitting by the fire and watching the rain slide through the trees. Two winters ago in Corvallis, Oregon, I was spending one of those rainy afternoons rereading Jarold Ramsey's collection of Northwest tales, *Coyote Was Going There: Literature of the Oregon Country*. The stories in that book are richly evocative of the range of humor and artfulness of the Northwest's oral tradition. In the volume's introduction Ramsey imaginatively re-creates a storytelling scene from two or three generations ago: the campfire, the fishing canoes outside the lodge, a circle of storytellers. Ramsey goes on in more sober tones to suggest that many of the stories, the art of reciting them, in fact, even the languages are slipping away, "lost like smoke through a smokehole." Unfortunately, to some degree, he is correct. And yet, I found myself vaguely troubled by yet another assertion of Native American literature and culture as "lost." To my students at Oregon State University, their images of American Indians tended to exist in the past tense. They pictured the proverbial scene of Chief Joseph stumbling through the snow along the Bitterroot. Their ideas of Indian art consisted of beadwork smelling of mothballs in heavy wooden cases at state museums.

I found disconcerting the notion that the American Indian was a vanishing relic, particularly in a region that boasted a healthy community of Native Americans. I wanted my students to be aware of the liveliness, of the continuity of American Indian culture, art, and literature. Indeed Ramsey himself, in his text's introduction, noted the importance of looking at Northwest American Indians in the present as well as future tenses:

> Inescapably, I have used the past tense here in trying to introduce their [American Indian] myths to general readers: but in dwelling so much in matters of tradition and pre- or mythic history, I do not want to imply that the continuities of Indian life, culture, and art have been broken. . . . Anyone who hopes

> to engage and cherish these stories should understand, if he is not Indian, that without taking pains to acknowledge the continuity of Indian life, its *futurity* as well as its history, he is in danger of merely sentimentalizing a rich native literature. Such sentimentality—"Lo! the poor Indian, exotic, pathetic, bound to a classical past, and safely in hand"—is ultimately vicious. It is a way of keeping a wise and gifted people in the place we have made for them, a way of continuing to ignore what they and their traditional literature might be giving us now."

Indeed, not only is the notion of the Vanishing American "vicious," it is simply false. Ramsey's book appeared in 1977, and in the decade that followed a number of the region's American Indian writers earned national acclaim. James Welch and Duane Niatum published continuously, and their work formed that backbone of courses in contemporary American Indian literature. Other writers such as Mary TallMountain, Earle Thompson, and Anita Endrezze became well known to editors of American Indian poetics. And across the region creative writing programs at the Universities of Washington and Oregon as well as at Eastern Washington State attracted young American Indian writers. One particularly articulate renunciation of the myth of "lost" Indian culture appeared in 1988 when Northwestern poet Chrystos published her first volume entitled *Not Vanishing*.

A decade after Ramsey's call for "futurity" in the region's Native American literature, I began work on an anthology of contemporary Northwest Native American literature. Initially, I did not set out to create a scholarly edition, although it is my hope that students and teachers of American Indian literature will turn to this volume from time to time. Rather, I have intended this volume as a celebration of the creativity, enthusiasm, and craft that marks literary efforts in the region. I want this volume to serve as an introduction to some of the finest writers in the Northwest today. For those readers who wish to continue their journey through American Indian literature of the region, I have included a bibliography at the end of this collection.

A regional presentation must always define its boundaries because the lines on the maps are never adequate. We redefine them ourselves, using geography, linguistic clues, or our instincts. I have followed the lead of editors such as Robert Frank, whose *Regionalism in the Northwest* defines the Northwest to include what is now viewed as the states of Oregon, Washington, British Columbia, Alaska, and east through Idaho and western Montana. Some have defined northern California as part of the region; others might question my inclusion of a section of Montana. Yet in the latter case, I was moved by the example of James Welch, a Blackfeet/Gros Ventre from Missoula who sees himself as a Northwestern writer, and the strong ties to Seattle that his work reveals seem to me to affirm his connection.

These issues of place and boundaries articulate a need to define loosely who I regard to be a "Northwestern writer." In preparing this collection I have thought about the category in three ways. First, I include those individuals who come from the region, whether or not they continue to reside here, and who feel that their writing continues to be moved by the spirit of the place. A second group consists of those artists who now reside in the Northwest and for the most part who have lived in the region long enough to call it home. Finally, I have decided to include a third group of writers who lived in the Northwest long enough to have felt personally affected by it. Jim Barnes is one example of this group. He wrote me once that his years as a lumberjack in Oregon were pivotal to his growth as a writer, and his poems in this volume seem to me to attest to his connection to the region. Ultimately, such decisions are deeply personal. I have tried in all cases to defer definition to the writers themselves.

As the project began to take shape, I realized that I wanted to include not only the work of well-known writers but as well to offer a place in the collection to a number of emerging writers. The idea of the old and new voices together seemed most appropriate. The well-known writers were easy to find. They tended to have university affiliations or editors who would forward their mail. It has been a greater challenge to find the best of the new voices. In 1987 and throughout 1988 I contacted all the creative writing programs in the region as well as editors of journals that frequently publish American Indian literature. Editors such as Joseph Bruchac (*Greenfield Review*), Larry Evers (Sun Tracks), and Brother Benet Tvedten (*Blue Cloud Quarterly*) have perhaps done more than anyone else to promote the work of this new generation of American Indian writers, and we are all in their debt. Closer to home, through her journal *Calyx*, Marguerite Donnally has continued to publish new work by women of color, and her efforts and dedication have been an inspiration to me. I wanted to insure that the volume would reflect the work of a wide panorama of Indian country, so I wrote as well to the cultural committees of many of the Northwest tribes requesting their assistance in identifying writers from their regions. And finally, the state arts commissions as well as cultural groups such as the Institute of Alaska Native Arts all spread the word. Yet perhaps the most effective networking came through the writers themselves. It seemed each person who wrote or called to submit work sent along the names of a few other writers. I was dazzled by the volume and talent of the submissions.

No anthology has room to publish as many poems and stories as an editor would hope. Yet I feel that *Dancing on the Rim of the World* does highlight the voices, moods, and vision not only of the region's finest Native American writers, but of the Northwest herself. I said earlier that I saw this book as an introduction, and I am pleased that even while this book has been in production, a number of outstanding publications have appeared. Robert Davis's *Soulcatcher*; Elizabeth Woody's *Hand Into Stone*; Jim Barnes's *La Plata Contata*, and Duane Niatum's *New and Selected Poems* are just a few of the new collections of poetry by Northwest Native American writers. Aside from individual volumes, the last couple of years have also seen new anthologies: Duane Niatum's *Harper's Twentieth Century Native American Poetry* includes the work of a number of Northwestern writers, and Joseph Bruchac has been working on an anthology of Native writers from Alaska. A complete list of books by contributors appears in section one of the bibliography.

Finally, perhaps the most significant literary development in the region has been the emergence of the Northwest Native American Writers Association. Already the group has published an attractive series of broadsides, and they have been organizing readings throughout the region. Currently, they are at work on a directory of the region's Native writers, and we can look forward to a number of new projects as they continue to encourage and promote literary activities throughout the Northwest.

As the manuscript neared completion, I asked Elizabeth Woody and Gloria Bird, two founding members of the Northwest Native

American Writers Association whether they might write a brief essay for this volume. It seemed to me most appropriate to have their words introduce this book for they stand in the center of the circle of Northwest Native literature. I think of Jarold Ramsey's vision of the campfire and the circle of storytellers back three generations ago. I am pleased to offer to readers a new circle of words and writers.

A. L.

Dancing on the Rim of the World

The Rim of the World

The Northwest, "the rim of the world," like the rest of the "New World" of centuries ago, is a complex place of diverse, original peoples, ecosystems, and masterworks of art and language. As Northwest Native Americans, our perception of the boundaries of our region are quite different from the generally accepted ones that recognize arbitrary state lines; the reaches of our language groups suggest a greater territory, which, expressed in present political boundaries, includes southern Alaska, southwestern Canada, Montana, Washington, Oregon, Idaho, western Nevada, and northern California.

Our lives are exceptional from the new Americans in that we can claim a heritage that involves no fewer than forty thousand years with this continent. For example, a site called Celilo Falls (Wyam) was one of the longest continuously inhabited sites in the Northwest, lived in for well over twelve thousand years. Although it now lies inundated by the backwaters of the Dalles Dam (1956), its omniscience is evident in writing by Native Americans of this region. Earle Thompson writes, "One of my poems 'Dancer' has a particular line that lingers: 'Dancing on the rim of the world' from this vantage point we can see the sky so blue and the water and the shoreline; we can see Celilo Falls; the fishing platforms, and we survive in harmony with our inner and outer natures." Celilo Falls of Earle Thompson's poetry illustrates how Native individuals *define* themselves through relationships that include one's associations with family, household, or village. As writers, also, we know our strengths are our native languages, histories, and traditions that respect what is shared in common.

It needs to be stressed here that by our (Native American writers') active participation in contemporary literature, we should recognize the simultaneous existence of a living ancestral literature that shines through the eclipse of non-Native chronicles. In this light we can understand why the *voice* of the Northwest is a tribal one, rooted as it is in the oratorical visions of accessible past leaders such as Smohalla, Chief Joseph, Chief Leschi, and Chief Tommy Thompson, to name only a few. Like the Aborigines of Australia who sing dream songs that describe to the listener the geography of their origins, we, too, have a land-shape in our stories and songs. You can hear this in the observances of land cycles in our Indian communities as we give thanks for life. The Plateau tribes, which we are most familiar with, have first fruits and first salmon ceremonies to offer communal respect and rejoice in the return of our relatives to nourish us. This continued interdependence with land may well be the only principle that will save our planet.

Our literature has suffered and our history has been misrecorded in poor translations. It has been stereotyped as "shamanic," "mythic," or "primal," and overall thought to be naive by the general population. Before we can address the literary merit of our work as Native American writers, we must first deconstruct the myths about us. In many anthologies of Native American literature we see the perpetuation of the myth of the Vanishing American. It is repeated consistently in the overattention given to "surrender speeches," as if oratory exists as a part of our past.

We are confronted with the continuation of this aspect in some Native American literature courses, which sometimes serve as the only introduction students have to Indian people's existence, past or present. We no longer live with the assumption that the efforts of ethnologists and the literary milieu have the exclusive responsibility to preserve, and therefore the right to *own*, our work. At the same time, we recognize there has been much responsible scholarship on our people. We ourselves must often look to archives or works of non-Native scholars in our personal research to document and study the taproot of our conditions, but through literature we have the opportunity to express some important concepts, not exclusively Native American or Northwestern, but imparted to us from the environment.

On the other hand, there are specific instances of cultural appropriation that weaken that healthy exchange. Recently Skamania County Historical Society registered the symbol of the well-known petroglyph of the lower Columbia River, Tsagaglalal (She Who Watches), for their trademark. They have claimed *ownership* of an image without sensitivity to the Indian people who acknowledge her in their legends. The Yakima Nation has stepped forward to protect and preserve its traditional cultural and religious interests in the petroglyph's image and has challenged the notion that such a figure can become a clichéd commercial instrument. It is not enough simply to recognize oratorical traditions. What is needed is an understanding from our perspective of why it is so important for us to remember.

In the Northwest we have a number of native scholars and teachers actively writing and teaching from the background of their traditions. Especially notable are Vi Hilbert, author of *Haboo*, a collection of Skagit legends; Allen P. Slickpoo, Sr., author of *Nee-Me-Poom Tit Wah Tit* (Nez Perce Legends); as well as Gail Tremblay of Evergreen State College; Elizabeth Cook Lynn, editor of *Wicazo Sa Review* (Eastern Washington University, Cheney, Washington); and Roger Jack of Eastern Washington University. These are only a few of the many Native American scholars who teach in our Northwest system of higher education. What compels us to continue to write and teach in colleges and universities, to study linguistics or learn old languages, is that, for us, the *traditional* storytellers, elders, and orators, still exist. As we continue to "write the voice down," we are in a position to shape the emerging patterns.

Non-Indians may find themselves uncomfortable facing the cultural suppression, disease, political repression, and dispossession that we have endured and often write about. These disturbing issues are not a part of the silent past, but extend into modern society. During the 1980s, for example, we have lived with active neo-Nazi cults, eviction of Indian families from traditional livelihoods, and Indian grave-robbing—all of which confront Indian writers of the Northwest. Writers and artists have always been a threat to tender ideologies. We accept this challenge, as writers traditionally have, knowing that socially, we represent a microcosm of situations that plague everyone throughout the world. Somewhere, someone will assert that suppression is not a reality in contemporary America. Yet, remember that in 1988 Father Ernesto Cardinal was denied entrance to this country to tour and read his poetry. The irony is that while we create in a political hotbed, we *can* choose to let politics ride shotgun. It is different for each writer, but it is still part of our serious literature to play upon the incongruities of our lives.

The urge has been to *write down* the old stories before the old people have gone, or *write down* the language while there are elders who speak it. Humishuma (1888–1936), or Crystal Quintasket, an Okanagon woman, gathered stories in her time from the elders, and worked on a dictionary of the dialects of the Okanagon. She is known for *Cogowea, The Halfblood* (1927), one of the first published novels by a Native American. Her book illustrates the dilemma of being a half-blood: one was not accepted fully by either group. This theme has repeated itself both literally and in literature, although we have come a long way since Humishuma's time. By pulling away from a trusting status with the United States and its imposing definitions of blood quantum, we are all in a sense "half-bloods," a metaphor for walking in two worlds. In writing, we are taking back control of our tribes and our lives.

Even though American culture freely borrowed Native American democratic concepts from the Great Laws of Peace of the Iroquois Confederacy to create the Constitution of the United States, it has continually ignored the fact that there are people of the original spirit among us: entire tribes whose prerogatives are for a free society and a livable environment for the forthcoming Seventh Generation. From the Arctic Circle to the tip of South America we have indigenous people dedicated to this cause, making a statement, be it in literature, or voiced orally in a Sundance ceremonial, in Canada or Montana, in a sweatlodge with Buddhist monks during the Long Walk of 1978, or lobbying in Congress to incite our generation to responsive self-government or land and wildlife preservation.

Already our central figures of legend, Coyote and Raven, are common cultural motifs in mainstream art. Archetypal, they still breathe through the facsimiles of the original trickster/changers, achieved in the pre-Euro-American traditions by the storyteller/poet. Some of our applications, perhaps, are direct crossovers from this old medium, but each of us reflects deeply upon the complexity of our indigenous status in the context of our lives and our literary craft. We have a responsibility to the movement that began centuries ago. Our issues arise from that ancient body of thought and extend outward. There is a resurgence of participation in the Longhouses, Smokehouses, traditional dances, and the arts. The force of this movement also extends to contemporary theater, dance, and art, which deserve contemplation in their connection to our literature. This connection, however, cannot be covered in this specific essay, except to mention that many of the writers that we represent from the region are also visual artists, actors, scriptwriters, and filmmakers. As Ward Churchill, the Creek-Cherokee social historian, pointed out during a packed discussion in a Portland bookstore in 1988, "Indians are the barometers of the country." At best, we exemplify the great hope and ability of people to turn disaster around. Our contemporary progression in literature is analogous to human development in myth: of becoming complete, reawakened within the laws of the universal. The making of symbols and images is directly entwined with our Northwest homeland, family, ancestors, their graves, teachings, and specific sites that mark our tenure. Literature, funneled through these channels, surfaces alive and wonderful for all our children. To highlight this aspect of our primal and universal function is to insure the integrity of our literature.

The light at the rim spreads from collectives and combinations of talent, that specific "injin-uity," to enrich our communities. Aboriginal consortiums, such as the one surrounding Theytus Books, LTD., whose most visible members include Viola Thomas and Janet Armstrong, work in association with En'Owkin Centre in British Columbia; The Institute of Alaska Native Arts in Fairbanks, Alaska; Press Gang Publishers, Vancouver, British Columbia (Chrystos's *Not Vanishing*); and the three-year-old Northwest Native American Writers Association of Portland, Oregon (*NWNAW Broadsides Collections*) exemplify Native American efforts to publish books that exist throughout the region.

The elders are sharing through people like Bruce Miller, Virginia Beavert, Allen P. Slickpoo, Sr., and P. Y. Minthorn—people who work silently, without acclaim, to collect stories and songs correctly. Virginia Beavert, as an example, compiled a text of legends and unselfishly gave the copyright to the Yakima Tribe.

We do not fail to recognize such efforts to inform one another. On the global level, Maori traditionalists visit Northwest Washington communities to build and race canoes in *Waterborne*, a native canoe project. Aboriginal radio broadcasters tour the Northwest to gather programs to air. This light is seen as part of a necessary shared spiritual culture that circles the globe, and sheds the "minority" veil in which history has draped us.

World interest in native culture is further illustrated in foreign language translations, groups of touring artistic emissaries, and medicine people crossing the oceans. Native American communities will prove an asset as our region moves to the forefront in a world economy that is now focused on the Pacific Rim. Major components of Northwest industries are inextricably tied to Indian lands. Many countries have interest in, and some sympathy for, Indian cultures by merit of our reputed ecological sense, and the "green trend" similarly embraces our aesthetics and philosophy. The overflow of this interest in our literature directs a growing awareness that could positively unite the dichotomous factions of Native and Nonnative, right and left, East and West. We believe it will be through our images, again, that we will meet as equals. The challenge we face today is whether to maintain our literature as *Indian*, that is, as this ethnic fragment, or to reclaim the original place of honor as participants of a dynamic cultural force.

We look to the future in anticipation of more films by Sandra Osawa. (*In the Heart of Big Mountain* was included in the Annual Rainbow Film Festival in Portland, Oregon, 1988.) There will be more productions of award-winning plays such as those by William Yellow Robe, Jr. (*Independence of Eddy Rose*). The wealth of native playwrights of the Northwest includes Ed Edmo (*Through Coyote's Eyes*) and Monica Charles, whose plays originated at the Institute of American Indian Arts in Santa Fe and were performed across the country by the nationally recognized Native American Theatre Ensemble. Bruce Miller tells myths at the Haystack summer workshops on the Oregon coast, and is part of the Dreamkeepers film productions. Our writers are visible in events, such as Bumbershoot in Seattle, the Portland Poetry Festival, the Portland Arts and Lectures Series, the Fishtrap Gathering in the Wallowas, and the Oregon Institute for the Literary Arts fellowships and awards. The applause, anthologies of prose and poetry, novels, awards to plays, film, and video have been earned by our Native writers as contemporary artists, not as ethnic constituents enriching a popular culture.

In this light contemporary Native American literature is a tribute to the keenness, tenacity, and intellect of our forebears. The many unheard voices, the invaluable record keepers of tribe and family, as well as the lesser known writers in this anthology deserve recognition as well. This is to cite the people who struggle alone to write what they have learned in their communities, but who may not consider themselves writers. They are possibly our most valuable asset, next to our children, in that they link our words from one generation to another .

We are greatly indebted to our "elders in the field," including James Welch, Mary TallMountain, Adrian C. Louis, Bill Oandasan, Nora Dauenhauer, Duane Niatum, Gladys Cardiff, Ed Edmo, Monica Charles, Liz Sohappy, Phil George, Ted Tomeo-Palmanteer,

Janet Campbell Hale, Agnes Pratt, and R. A. Swanson, to name a few. They are the founders of a heritage of fine writing from the Northwest. From Humishuma's time to the present, we are now related through the strength of their voices "dancing on the rim of the world."

ELIZABETH WOODY AND GLORIA BIRD

Northwest Native American Writers' Association
Portland, Oregon

JIM BARNES

Jim Barnes is of Choctaw-Welsh descent. He lumberjacked for ten years in Oregon's Willamette Valley. After finishing a Ph.D. at the University of Arkansas, he joined the faculty at Northeast Missouri State University, where he has edited *The Chariton Review* for the past fourteen years. In 1980 he was awarded a Translation Prize from the Translation Center of Columbia University for *Summons and Sign: Poems by Dagmar Nick*. His books of poetry include *The American Book of the Dead* (University of Illinois Press, 1982), *A Season of Loss* (Purdue University Press, 1985) and *La Plata Cantata* (Purdue University Press, 1988). He held a Rockefeller Bellagio Fellowship for the spring of 1990.

Commenting on his tribal affiliation, Jim noted, "There is no Choctaw tribe, only a widely scattered Choctaw nation, individuals all. I am Choctaw by blood, by my small knowledge of the language, and by an inherited love of horses and watermelon."

ONE FOR GRAND RONDE, OREGON

"I gave them fire . . . , blind hope."
—AESCHYLUS, *Prometheus Bound*

Ghosts of dead loggers haunt the night
where General Sheridan drove the light
into the last warring tribes. Grand Ronde
lies lead under the hoot-owl moon.

Indians and loggers die here still.
Years ago Big Moose drank his fill
of rotgut, told it like it was,
told them all to go to hell because

they were. The mountain called him up,
shook his senses clean, and let him jump.
Others still can hear his dark call
the nights the sky begins to fall.

No one has the guts to say where's hope.
Crow's a poor savior anymore. Croak
and feathers made the night. But now
what's left? The flayed god and the scowl

on the face of Spirit Mountain. The moon
is never right: the blood's too soon
for sacrifice and the constant rain
pounds like a wedge into the brain.

There's not one soul left in this town
who does not try to pray the frown
off the stone face the mountain's made
of: give us this day, god knows we've paid.

AT THE BURN ON THE OREGON COAST

The hills' heads lie bodiless on the mist,
ghost ships deadlocked on a ghostly sea, masts

rigid and dark against the faint ashen light of dawn.
Among last trees, the ringed fingers of sun are slow to sound

the depths of gimcrack trunks. The flagged trail
wakes to the wayward gamming of jays. The last wail

of an owl sinks away: the night bird battens
down fast against the day. Now the running wind

wafts through the crossed bones of trees and beasts, quick
as needles to thread the hills together, to stitch away the dark.

NEAR CRATER LAKE

Between hill and river the trail
forks, edges deep in stone only
shadows know, and only the stones
can say which way my fathers took.
Steps and lives have worn away
the mountain agates' chalky maps
so I can say they went this way
or that and knew the sounds upon
the land, knew too the rush of wings.
The hill fork leads to a sky beyond
the hill, the river fork down water
fast with rainbows and quick jacks.

Ways my fathers walked are things I
learn from hard stones. I lift my arms
and hold the bear, the bull, the lost
maidens, and the hunter mad for game;
I make a prayer for the drawn bow

to send beyond the sun and down
the last dark corridor of sky:
old fathers, when you come again,
old fathers, tell me once again
why the path forks and the river
runs fast with fish to homes beneath
another sky, homes beneath the sea.

CONTEMPORARY NATIVE AMERICAN POETRY

For one thing, you can believe it:
the skin chewed soft enough to wear,
the bones hewn hard as a totem
from hemlock. It's a kind of scare-
crow that will follow you home nights.
You've seen it ragged against a field,
but you seldom think, at the time,
to get there it had to walk through hell.

GLORIA BIRD

Gloria Bird is a native of Washington state and member of the Spokane Tribe. She has attended the Institute of American Indian Arts in Santa Fe, New Mexico and lived in the Southwest for several years. She has been published in *Fireweed*'s issue on Native women. Currently, she is one of the First Circle members of the Northwest Native American Writers Association, and she is an English major at Portland Community College in Portland, Oregon. She is a single mother of five, and between school, work, and home, she is working on her manuscript.

Bare Bone Winter

In this bare bone winter the woman splits kindling to start a fire. Her chipping axe, a steady beat, echoes in the stillness half a mile down the road. She works unhurried, honed to the texture of each piece of wood. With little pressure, her sharpened axe slips down the grain. *Somewhere, a Trader is selling Indian finger-bone in an old basket with pottery shards.* Sweet wood smell rises thick in the open shed. She smooths an amber stone of treegum between her teeth, a small concession to hunger. *The people were running from Cavalry fire.* Over barbed-wire fence, the neighbor's horses clip their hooves into crusted snow, nose into stiff skeleton grasses for something more to eat. *A woman placed her baby in cradleboard in the crook of tree for safety.* She exhales a warm cloud into her hand, hangs her axe by its head on two nails in the wall of the shed, finished. *The babyboard grew into and part of the huge Y of branches, knifed through the heart of tree.* She bends to pick up her wood people, puts them into a box, carries in her kindling to start the fire. The sting of winter flames on her cold cheeks. She listens to the cracking and spitting dry kindling meal she feeds the fire with. *After sixteen hundred miles, Joseph surrendered the Wallowas forever.* Bones scatter like the hand of winter, ghost that comes back for warming marrow, or evidence.

NINE MONTHS WAITING

I am waiting in this my mountain home
for the child to be born.
Stroking the curve of belly
I push a bulb of elbow or foot
and feel him flutter within me.
The slow fire crackles in the stove,
dances in the background
of these thoughts
of my spring child, my sun.

The mountain pines, the clear skies,
the clean air, and even the coyotes I've claimed,
who howl too close some nights,
give me strength.
wonder if I will ever tell
the child why we are here,
or about the time
I nearly killed a dream I had
who was only a man
and that when I awoke alone and afraid
it was his child who rocked in me?

The pain persists
as I watch cloud formations
from my window.
I think of living and dying
the way pregnant women do
and pray for this to be
the last pain I will bear
from that other time and place,
but more, from that man.

GLADYS CARDIFF

Born in Browning, Montana, Gladys Cardiff attended school in Seattle, Washington. She studied with Theodore Roethke and Beth and Nelson Bentley at the University of Washington.

Mrs. Cardiff has participated in the Poetry in the Schools Program, and various workshops including the Women's conferences at the University of Washington and the University of Puget Sound. She has given readings at numerous public schools, libraries, and a number of universities. As well she was invited to read at the Seattle Bumbershoot Festival.

Her book, *To Frighten A Storm*, received the Governor's Writers Award for a first book upon its publication in 1976 by Copper Canyon Press. She has been selected by the Seattle Arts Commission as a prize recipient in 1985 and 1986. In 1988 she was a co-recipient of the University of Washington's Louisa Kerns Award for literary endeavors.

Mrs. Cardiff's poems have been widely published in journals as well as in anthologies including *Carriers of the Dream Wheel* (Harper & Row), *The Remembered Earth* (Red Earth Press); *That's What She Said: An Anthology of Contemporary Native American Women* (Indiana University Press), and *Harpers Twentieth Century Native American Poetry* (Harper & Row).

Her Tribal enrollment is with the Eastern Band of Cherokees, Cherokee, North Carolina.

ENOCH SPEAKS OF OMENS

Sge'. Listen. This is what I have seen.
The water in Black Lake has darkened.
Weavers go there to dip their cane
as they did *hilahi*, long ago.
The cane is clean and supple floating
just below the surface.
The lake looks like a black bowl designed
with pale, white lattices around its rim.
By morning, the cane is a dusky color,
bluish purple like big-headed clover.
Many baskets now are woven
with the blue path of loneliness.

Sge.' For every river
there is a recent happening.
Long Person is disturbed and boils
with water spouts and whirlpools.
The Tuskegee, Oconoluftee, Hiwassee,
they are disgorging from the deep wells
of their being as if paying up
  arrearages.
Boots, buckets, boats, even bodies
of small animals litter their banks.
The grass along the river's edge glints
with the bronze coins of sunperches.
I remember going to water
wearing the red stripes of purification.
Long Person gave power, the strength
of all that had come before and was to come.
Perhaps the rivers are thirsty for the taste of bloodlines.

Have you not seen how the sycamore
and bushy hedge are bewitched?

How, at any hour, even when the wind
holds itself still in a deep breath,
a part of the tree will move?
Only one part, one section in the middle
or lower to the ground, will shake its leaves
making them jump like startled green fish.
No bird or squirrel hides in the branches,
no dog scratches his back on the limbs below.
The tree is feeling some spirit passing through
and quakes like the guilty heart
of an impassive man.
The leaves hiss like a sudden gust
of rain against window glass,
or as if salt from a giant shaker
was pouring through the greenery,
cascading from curve to curve
with the sound of time being shaken.
What of the rocks and black roads
stunned and bare under the noon day sun.
Nothing slides through the cheat grass
or sleeps coiled in the dumpyard.
The snakes have disappeared. The bull
and black, the red racer, the copperhead,
all are having a congress somewhere
where the paths are unknown,
where they can't be found.

Sge'. I am an old man and these are small signs.
You will say they are the imaginings
of one who longs for the ancient times.
There is more respect for the words of an old man
if he doesn't dwell too long on those things
of magic. But, I say to you,
sge', listen, something is coming.

It is the Fabulous One,
it is the Great Uktena.*

*The Great Uktena, the "keen-eyed" is a mythic, Cherokee being. Immense, serpent-like, it has a third eye on its crest that is fatal to any who gaze into it. This third eye is a crystal that can be used with great caution by a medicine man. The Great Uktena lives in remote places in the mountains or in deep lakes and rivers.

PRETTY BIRD

While morning lifts its green blanket,
he waits, radiant, a little god
in the emerald light of his cage.

He wants out. He wants the height
of his perch. His impatience is charged
and crackles in a plumage of blue volts.

Yellow eyes stare from the ornate
mask of his face with its black chin
and ebony beak. His cheeks are white

and warm, like a Japanese dancer's skin.
Little black feathers, singular and distinct
as the dark acts we choose, stripe each cheek.

As I unlock his cage, I wonder if we wear
our demerits in some ancestral grain
like the reptilian yellow of his stare.

He climbs the pole, his feathers shimmering
like green leaves moving in a constant wind,
or water rippling in a cape of blue harmonics.

He is made for the tallest trees.
His back is blue sky, and his breast
the gold gap of sun through branches.

But here, the ground below him is littered
like a boneyard with wood chips and husks.
Clearly, he is excavating the wood

from beneath himself. One day, the perch
will split and separate, and he will know
the delicious sway of mountain branches

and abandonment. Two sharp terminals
will charge the void. And he will fall
the way a crippled bird must, in a long

downward spiral, his one clipped wing
pivotal.

VICTOR CHARLO

Victor A. Charlo is a Bitterroot Salish parent, poet, philosopher, theologian and teacher. He works as a counselor with the Confederated Salish and Kootenai tribes at the Kicking Horse Job Corps in Montana.

FLATHEAD RIVER CREATION

for the students of the Two Eagle River School

You say
old days fold into one another
and new days seem the same.
Yet each moment shifts with sun,
nothing will be the same as this:

when wind breathes the Flathead alive,
you are the center this instant
for all, you are the creation
of the universe one more time.

DIXON DIRECTION

Directions are simple here.
Geese know where to go
and eagles fly. Yet sometimes
you get lost on wrong roads.

Then

when you come to school,
you seek from this high window
and find living river, red willow,
white aspen, old juniper and pine.

This is you.

And bright, clay cliffs fix the stars.

FROG CREEK CIRCLE

for my family, especially Jan

Mountains so close we are relative.
Creek so cold it brings winter rain.

We return to warm August home,
Frog Creek, where I've lived so long
that smells are stored, opened only
here. This land never changes, always
whole, always the way we want it to be,
yet we always come back
to check our senses or to remember
dreams. We are remembered today in circles
of family, of red pine, of old time chiefs,
of forgotten horses that thunder dark stars.

These are songs that we come to this day,
soft as Indian mint, as strange as this day.

THE MILLTOWN

for Anne Marie Jehle

We miss Garnet soon after we get
on golden road as we talk about how
we see the world. Our job today—to honor
Hugo's memory by stopping at places
he saw and wrote about. Garnet ghosts
are tricky.

Milltown Union Bar (Laundromat
and Cafe) felt strange until we went in. There
was something wrong yet right about that bar
still called Harold's Club. Harold tried to get fancy
and changed the name on us. Dick wrote a poem
about the old name, place that I truly know, and I
open in at Milltown.

So, Anne Marie, I bring
you here to see these heads and this bad
painting. The crossed swords gone or hidden.
The rest is here. We order draft beer
like Dick and I would do. I read his poem
to you. That moment would have been fine
if it ended there, but it didn't.

No, the guy with a snoot full sitting next to me asks,
"What you got there?" pointing to Hugo's
book. I happily show him the poem,
and he reads. He laughs and asks where
he can get a copy of the book.
I tell him this particular one
is probably out of print. I can't close
the door. He tells me to show the poem
to the bartender. She reads long and smiles.
She asks if she can copy the poem.
I'm glad. She buys us "two scoops," as we
used to call them. She says, "mugs." I think
of Dick's line as she writes on that yellow pad:
"You need never leave. Money or a story brings
you booze." Or a memory, I think. The spelling
queen bee told us the word laundromat
is spelled wrong. Bartender, you and I act
as if it's still there, not gone.

Everything
else was there that day in disarray. They saved
the heads even if Harold tried to make
his bar that elegant club where people
from Missoula would fly by freeway.
We came. Dick, Annick, Dave, me, students
and what about the time we shot part
of the first movie on that Saturday
night.

And, Anne Marie, these memories
all have meaning not just for me
but for you, now, not just because you
are my friend, but because the word burns
with first fire. We are these stories now
as sure as Dick and I would sing you
now, then to magic time, to those first
safe places we find growing up. And now
we burn yes, we sing yes to world we find
in us.

CHRYSTOS

Chrystos was born in San Francisco in 1947 to a Menominee father and a Lithuanian mother. She has lived in the Northwest for about ten years close to the Suquamish reservation. She is "proudly uneducated & politically involved with the struggle at Big Mountain & with SalmonScam." She works as a maid to support herself. Her collection of poems, *Not Vanishing*, was published by Press Gang (Canada) in 1988.

I HAVE NOT SIGNED A TREATY WITH THE UNITED STATES GOVERNMENT

especially for Celeste George

nor has my father nor his father
nor any grandmothers
We don't recognize these names on old sorry paper
Therefore we declare the United States a crazy person
  nightmare   lousy food   ugly clothes   bad meat
  nobody we know
No one wants to go there   This US is theory   illusion
terrible ceremony   The United States can't dance   can't cook
  has no children   no elders   no relatives
They build funny houses no one lives in but papers
  Everything the United States does to everybody is bad
No this US is not a good idea   We declare you terminated
  You've had your fun now go home we're tired   We signed
no treaty   WHAT are you still doing here   Go somewhere else and
  build a McDonald's   We're going to tear all this ugly mess
down now   We revoke your immigration papers
  your assimilation soap suds   your stories are no good
your colors hurt our feet   our eyes are sore
  our bellies are tied in sour knots   Go Away Now
  We don't know you from anybody
You must be some ghost in the wrong place   wrong time
  Pack up your toys   garbage   lies
We   who are alive now
  have signed no treaties
Burn down your stuck houses   your sitting
  in a nowhere gray glow   Your spell is dead
Go so far away we won't remember you ever came here
  Take these words back with you

MEDITATION FOR GLORIA ANZALDUA

On my forehead a bird in flight going places I can't see
feathered in light my whole body aches & pulls following
a tide
Moon has become my lover   lulls me with phosphorescent hands
her hair tangles mine like roots
As far as my heart reaches water breathes silver fish swimming
in my fingers to food of colors
Each stone in my shoe a reminder that I've so little time
beauty is so vast   I've so much more to get away with before
there is no more
with a hunger like fat red buds on brambles etched in frost
hunger like winter mallards combing breakers for life
hunger   that burns me infernos hungry for early spring waiting
in earth hungry for a shape I alone can make
Wanting to blend water & fire
Paint a deeper surface where we can surge
I want to take our breath away
like this eagle diving for a shrew
I want to go where all
the wings are

DEAR MR. PRESIDENT

I am a woman with 3 children, a husband who has been out of work
for 18 months & no place to go
I am one of 400 families Emergency Housing has turned away
this month
The 399 others are no consolation to me
This is an emergency
Mr. P. I am a mother of two who lives with my mother who can no
longer work
Someone reported to welfare that I was working
My checks have been temporarily stopped pending investigation
I think my ex-boyfriend's mother called them for spite
because I don't have a job
although I have submitted over 200 resumes in the last year & a half
We got evicted Emergency housing can't find us anything
This is an emergency
Hey Mr. Prez My boyfriend was beating me and the kids so bad
I just had to get out before one of us was killed
The battered women's is full & so is emergency housing
The worker said she'd already turned away 377 others this month
We're living in my car & cooking at my mother's studio apartment
in the old people's housing This is an emergency
400 times in one city that bother to try to fix it times 12 months
is a class of people
It is worse in other towns
When we have no place to live
Dear Mr. Pay Attention Now
we are not in economic recovery
We are in an emergency

WINTER EVENING

in the northern mountains
the moon is a silver turtle
moving slowly through stars

OUT THE TOP I GO

for Elizabeth Woody

leave my body like an autumn leaf head straight for the
rolling cloud people sing laugh juicy with it
whirl round till I'm dizzy
hot with sky bread Jump from blue to yellow to night
go see the moon Stick some stars in my teeth & hair
race a thunderbolt lightening streak
Grow a horse to gallop through the sunrise flying
into some birds with a feast to share
Go out the bottom of the bowl
cruising down to black holes in a racy convertible
hair slicked back looking for
trouble & something to drink
Turn into a buffalo munching on prairie sky
tell the sun a joke she laugh so hard she fall over
unexpected darkness Just a volcano
Hard
to come back here
after all that fooling around

IN THE GRIEF RIVER

No fish swim death an overdue bill third notice no where
to turn hanging
sheets on the line I shoulder away tears for you or more for me
Driving to work tears I imagine various excuses to disguise red
eyes but they don't ask I tell a few women that you're diagnosed
with spinal bone cancer Their stiffness kills me I'm not
supposed to talk about this Even you agree as you go fishing
don't want
the creel of my questions needs demands What a pain in the ass I
am You shout at me under your breath
Of course you'll let me know what's
but if you tell me you might overhear & then what
Not sure whether to pray for your life I wonder if you want it
Numb
& cracked since your mother & Anita died so close together maybe
you think you can't go on without their dawns in your eyes
Not my death I'm stiffly polite Wait for you to say what
you need every impulse in my body aches to make love to you for
months chase off chemotherapy
shouting like a bag lady gone round the bend
screaming for the blood of jesus which is against us
everyone dying all the time every moment I'm not supposed
to need you this much
Where are my casual shoes & coat? how will I go to the
hellish florist any more this year
order flowers under neon lights choking as I explain
white roses please her favorite or beg for dogwood which was hers
& was not available settling for something obscene called a
spring basket
absurdity radiating from my checkbook the clerk dead set against
my grief
wishing that coffee break would hurry up & come
How will
we ever have a cup of coffee again talk of nothing with such
comfort

as though we could depend on sunrises & each other
how many more graves before I'm one   Must be brave for you
Brave too long my basket frayed   I fall through gaps
grief is slow water
drip that cuts stone   swimming against the current nothing
to spawn
Where are the old wicker rockers on a twilight porch where
we planned to be old ladies chortling about our pasts   will it come
to a time when all I am is remembering deaths until I long
for mine to be born
Here is a photograph I took of you when we were lovers
Bending over the pier looking for fish a yellow handkerchief
sprouts gaily from your back pocket
your brown face & hands warm against the gray wood
your blue jeans so soft & old   one of the best pictures I've ever
taken   always meaning to send you a copy & forgetting
Not a fish I have no idea where I'm going
my sheets smell of lavender & salt spray   you could come here &
go fishing for salmon everyday
you could stay with me until   you could let me
memorize you   record your every word   follow you   let me cling
let me cry let me wail   you'd rather avoid all that
so would I in your place
I stare at my hands which can't cure cancer
still alive & thrashing
No roses   my skin salty in the grief river

JO WHITEHORSE COCHRAN

Jo Whitehorse Cochran (Lakota/Norwegian) lives in Seattle, Washington. She holds an M.A. in Creative Writing from the University of Washington. She feeds and clothes herself by working in the Office of Management and Budget for the City of Seattle. She is coeditor of *Changing Our Power: An Introduction to Women's Studies* (Kendall-Hunt, 1987).

Her passions in life are mountain biking and hanging out with Bob the Cat. What concerns her most is healing the planet and ourselves as individuals and peoples. She accomplishes this through being a Reiki practitioner and Seichim master. Her poetry rises from that commitment to healing the earth and the song of the grandmothers returning.

HALFBREED GIRL IN THE CITY SCHOOL

are you Mexican
are you Italian
are you Chinese
are you Japanese
    spic   wetback   greaseball   slant-eye
    you are dark enough to question
    you are light enough to ask
    you have near black hair   brown eyes
    and speak   slow-english
    we are blonde   blue eyed
    and wear store bought sweaters skirts or pants
    you are in homemade clothes   out of style
    we circle round   you   and   your sister
    you hug your sister close   she's small   and even darker
    we kick   we tug   at braids and coats
    we pull   "I'm Indian!" out of you

    the social worker wants
    you to describe your family
    she asks
        does your father beat you
        does your mother
        does your father drink
        does your mother
        do you hate your parents
        do you cry
    tell me   tell me   do you
    like the reservation better
    are you ashamed in the classroom
    when you wet your pants
        why don't you speak up
        why don't you get excused
        why don't you go at recess
    tell me   tell me   speak!

you stare out the window
turn an alphabet block in your hands
speak english speak english
the social worker caws
outside Canadian geese pass through your immediate sky
six in an arc going south
if you were a Changer like Star Boy
you could fly with those long-necks
but you must stay and look out this window

Grandma's words pound in your head
they want to strip us of our words
they want to take our tongues
so we forget how to talk to each other
  you swallow the rock
  that was your tongue
  you swallow the song
  that was your voice
  you swallow you swallow
  in the silence

FIRST OF FEBRUARY, NEW SNOW

Each sunset or rise is ordinary until we begin
to let our bodies see, until vision melds
with our spirits—to let us see in clarity
the burning orange of the madrona's peeled bark,
the mute blues of the hills across the Sound,
the incandescence of light behind gray clouds,
as day lessens into evening, and we feel ease,
the slow-closing of this cyclic movement
in our bodies, in our blood. We come to find
ourselves inextricably tied to this planet,
to the land before us, beneath us,
and we learn that living is never ordinary,
just deceptive in its directness,
like our bodies remembering our own breath.

LOVER'S NOTE

In bed we have left our enraptured bodies.
In the house our comfort, still mixed
with shy glances. As our seed coats
crumble, fall away, we open
and the braiding of our dance
has just begun. But, I tell you,
I have danced for rain,
for the ending of a season,
for the coming of light,
for the joy in my body/spirit,
for my coming womanhood,
for the singing of my spirit song,
yet never before for love,
for the heart songs of my own—
tempo, shake, tremor and flight—
we have begun such a full dance.

FROM MY GRANDMOTHER

(1913–1970)

You were talking   to my blood
in those years   before my memory
was awake.   When I had no one's language
yet   not Lakota   not Salish
not English

You were talking   me into life
and knowing.   Giving me colors
the thin gray   of pin feathers
on a redtail hawk   for blizzard sky
I would never see.   Dakota sky
just before   a white out.
Your midnight blue blanket   each end a light

with a mountain design   yellow to red,
these were candle flames   and the August night.

You were making sense   of things
in image   and textures
stories of Old Ones   Changers
and the Lakota   I can only find
in dreams   in visions.
Grandmother   are we searching
out   each other   you and I?
Or am I just   remembering
from you   from my blood.

NEARING WINTER

The Fool torn out of me by nearing winter,
needs the gathering of bay leaves, rose hips and comfrey.
Small bundles for survival through the moon of changing seasons.
I've been leaning, on edge, uncertain as a river,
for days trying to change course, to split the gravel bank.

Just don't scold me for this, these crazy connections
for my language of life.
A Fool rips out of me hissing,
"West!   West!   This is all there is!"
We can't be pushed any farther.
I can't.   Fool quick as Coyote bursts from my body,
runs in the rage of a head wind hollering, "This is all!"

I scramble after.   Haul her in by hair, neck and teeth
clamped around my arm.   Try to calm her.
Convince her, I hadn't forgotten her.
We scream and cry at this woman
who refuses to hold together.

ROBERT DAVIS

Robert Davis's tribal affiliation is Tlingit on his father's side. During his childhood his family spent part of each year in Michigan where his mother's family came from, while they spent the summers fishing in Kake, Alaska. In 1964 the family moved permanently to Kake where Robert became interested in Tlingit culture and art.

Davis makes a living as an artist. In addition to writing poetry, Robert also paints, carves wood, and teaches woodcarving workshops. Robert uses his writing as well as his visual art to express "the hopes and despair, the loss of traditional values, the pain of acculturation, and the flavor of the people and history of the place . . ." His poems have been published in *Raven's Bones*, *Journal of Alaska Native Arts*, *Orca Anthology*, *In the Dreamlight: 21 Alaskan Writers* as well as in the *Harper's Anthology of Twentieth Century Native American Poetry*. A volume of his poetry, *Soulcatcher*, was published by Ravens Bones Press in 1986.

SOULCATCHER

Far from the scent of crackling spruce,
far from throbbing sealskin drum,
into space, into wind,
wild hair flying,
old man sings
across the endless dark;
the man who leaves himself
cross-legged, hollow and still.
Medicine man. Soulcatcher.

In the short sharp ripples of firelight
painted carvings weave and snap
designs on the bentwood box
that holds the mystical charms,
soulcatcher amulets,
magic rattles.

Animal people, ocean people,
this is how he brings them back.
The air begins to move in them.
Thick men in cedar bark.
Incantation. Song, dance, story.
He could capture your soul if he had to.

The trees know.
They know how easy it is
to disappear forever, to sink
into fire and wind.
How a drifting figure
now wears a mask
of ash and bone
outside the village
that still feels air moving.

LEVELING GRAVE ISLAND

Some of the arms flew
up to where legs belong. Some
thighs smashed to ribs.
A few skulls smiled into their own pelvis.

Not a hundred years ago
the placement of bones, each particular
stance was the position for entering death country.
Broken knees and elbows to fit to chests,
placed on the platform
that floated back to earth evenly in time.

Bodies churn and roil in the earth.
The giant spruce, the eagle trees
the points of reference go up in smoke.
Nothing is so random.
We lose our direction.
I watch this destruction daily.

Gravemarkers donated to museums.
Trees explode.
The dozer that was ferried across
has leveled the entire island.
The living destroy the dead,
as the dead claim the living.
Like going off into the distance,
growing smaller and vanishing,
like rituals without origins,
like this island that never was and always will be.

INTO THE FOREST

for Steve Brown

Here heavy boughs hanging
with strands of withes
and wispy goatsbeard fungus
take the place of sky.

So dim and mystical
I hear legends whispered
from way back
behind each tree, each cedar
straining toward totem,
barkskin twisting and unwrapping
exposes bold formlines, curled
to knots like whorls on fingers.

Grain takes off to branches, and beyond
imagination.

Everything rises
from mere roots
anchored in the brown
bone of the earth.
Beneath the silence of moss
a mute voice
begging for voice.

A carver, I listen with hands.
Forest creatures hesitate—
all senses wide open.

DANGER POINT, BAINBRIDGE ISLAND

You lead me into approaching night
down to eelgrass reefs,
leave behind safe houselights.

Channel markers' strobes
punctuate loud thoughts.

Between each pulse
the red lid of the sky
slowly closes, blinks.
Then we like irritating specks
are suddenly gone.

All that remains,
a deepening trail,
naked footprints
so close together
in the mudflats on Danger Point.

Afterimage of bone-colored moon
shaken from its mooring
by waves folding over and over.

I make out my voice
going on about the painters, the poets.
Derelicts who straggled all the way to death.
About the channel markers.
All the intrepid seamen
who have vanished just-like-that.

Now the odor of seaweed begins to rise.
Now the madronas reclaim all light.
A cry from the invisible seabird
echoes off the deep wall of darkness.

This is the point
the sea draws up on either side.
At this point time hangs momentarily,
then surges around you.
This is any time,

the point where I start to whisper
how this feels all too familiar,
that we might turn back, now

while the tracks that led us here
are still recognizable
as our own.

DROWNING

We think we are safe
on this beach, on this dreamscape,
luminescence washing the shores.
Lowtide odors; sulfur clams, kelpbed.
We come out of the fog
and cling to the fire,
the shell of our own voices
at the edge of the woods,
at the edge of the sea,
somewhere between these two kinds of darkness.

I remember now
stories of that country
where drowning men end up,
urged there by Land Otter People—
the Kooshdaakaa.
They take you ashore, they look familiar.
The village itself looks familiar.
Not even surprised at your otter-whistle voice,
you begin to live by your one sense left,
insatiable hunger. You scour tidepools
for mussels and barnacles,
the flats for clams; you crawl.

Ee! Look at you!
You wouldn't recognize yourself,
hair matted and hanging
over wild roving eyes,
lips stretched in grimace.

You stink.   You sniff.
Fear comes off of you.
Half-awake, waiting for light
shapes transform. Everything catches our breath.
Listen:

down there
cockle shells clatter,
a low pitched whistle
I think is calling.

DEBRA CECILLE EARLING

Debra Earling is a member of the Confederated Salish and Kootenai Tribes of the Flathead Reservation in Montana. She is currently a graduate student in English at Cornell University.

WINTER KEEPS

"If I were the middle winter month
like January, I would freeze all
the unborn babies in the mother's
womb." Indian February on the Flathead

A cold wind cracks your spine humming.
Your wet breath puffs smoke-dry from dawn to dusk.
        Cottonwood curves from shrill wind
        Stinging its branches.
Swollen stomach pulls tight at the curve of your ribs.
Looking to hills the color of clean deer-bone scraped cold
Your hands follow your belly.

He is hunting in valleys swollen with snow.
You are venison hungry,
                Huckleberry hungry.
                                Hungry as the wet mouths of birds.
The tips of his arrows wrapped with your hair,
You imagine deer liver warm with placenta
                Chokecherries red on the branch.

Snow buries the river like sleep.
You remember old stories of Winter unborn babies:
        Feet freeze first
        Then fingers stiffen and you begin to hunger
        For each cold kick thumping, before
        Stillness settles
        And only shivers stir your womb,
At night you huddle the smoldering fire.
Listen: Branches crack like bone.
                Ice-skin moans on the river.
Your hands follow the tight curve of your belly.

You remember Autumn, the deep warm
Channel of water moving
Pulling your hair clean,
Trees turning to fire
        In Autumn you gathered wood

Slept hot beside the base-blue tongues of flame
Burning buckskin tamarack.
Your hands followed the swell of your belly.

You wake cold, lift the skin back from shelter.
You break ice at the river.
Breaths float cold in deep water.
You gulp breath, rise clean, skin burning hot.
You think of summer, fields bright with Camas
Wind warm as birth.
Through river willows you see
Heat from your fire rising
Like a cold ghost over shivering aspens.

SUMMER HUMMING 1946

Loretta Two Teeth was found without blood
Shot once in the chest close range
In the hills above Polson.
Summer was a hot voice that year
A voice that lifted dry weeds to tumble
To fences humming wire.
And the grass was humming too
Humming over her as morning
Pulled a dawn white sky to dust.

Nattie Trout said that day
You could hear something moving through grass
The sound rocks make rubbing
Red cheat to fire.
Loretta Two Teeth quiet to sky.
Death rattled weeds on its way to the river.

Josephine Weaselhead was in Browning playing
Stickgames. She said she saw Loretta
Plain as day
Three days after Loretta had died.

Loretta Two Teeth opened her palms before she bid
Showed Josephine the two black bones.
Wind hummed the fields.
When Josephine walked home
Footsteps rattled the weeds behind her.
In Browning no one slept.

Nattie Trout said stand by the Juniper. Listen.
Magpies called the river blood.
It was 1946. Above every bar
In every big and little town hung one sign
Barring Indians and dogs.
Blood slept dry in the heat of women dying.
A voice moved through dry weeds
Humming the sound of women splitting wood.
Women spitting blood
Humming summer wind through grass.
Grandmothers you thought were dead
Hide behind trees
Knowing death
Sleeps close to rivers
The wet lips of lovers.
Fists cleanse the bones of women's ribs.
Loretta Two Teeth left the sound of breath
To Magpies.
Death is the hum of summer wind.
Death is the rattle in the weeds.
It is summer humming.

MONTANA BURIAL WIND

This summer a wind hums cottonwood dry
As your old-man neck. You plant
Four rows of cheat grass in an open field,
Scatter milkweed seeds kicking
Dust to the sun pulling

Wind to burial.
Here your days sleep long as boredom.
The town grows like wind on the horizon.
Each curve of the highway is a spine going nowhere.

In Montana, they told you fields wouldn't grow.
You'd die
        In God's open country wagging
        Dull fists to sky.
The bastards didn't lie.
When the barn burned down
Smoke smothered the old gelding.
Your wife became hard as mud-packed dust,
Said, "It wasn't good for nothing anyway."
You cried for the smoldering carcass.
She fanned the stink of chicken feathers to sky.
When you cuffed your hand to your brow
And found wrinkles,
You decided to move on.

Some mornings you walk through white weeds
To town, pass the four crosses
At Ravalli   that bridge the dead
To dust.
At the Buffalo you drink a cold belly to summer
Forget about planting.

Once you asked in the dust-dark bar
About the crosses, their rusted necks
Dead-dull with flowers. And the sons of bitches
Told you a story that made you remember
All your little sorrows:
                        The day your dog ran the highway
                        Lost to wind.
                The dull spine ache
                The clean crack of the windshield
                From the deer you hit in Autumn.

And that old memory,
The one you had forgotten,
When your wife planting
Stuck a hoe to buried bees
And miscarried the son
You had hoped for.

You drank.
They told you of the red-haired woman smoking
Cigarettes and tires from Mission
The way her car hit, splitting. The Indian girls
Scattered the bridge
Sliced slick to slivers,
Dripped dreams dry to the Jocko.
It was years ago,
Forty years you drink back
Old ghosts like sleep cupped in hearts.
Indian girls never haunt here.
Like hope they shine the highway every beer.

Dusk brings in ranchers who have planted
More rows of winter wheat just to sit
Still to your stories. And you tell them
Gloating, of the time you walked in August sun,
Head held high in wheat,
In Idaho, before your daughter
Died near Hope.

They will listen too, poor bastards,
While wind pulls dust over fields
Closing open ground.

SUMMER OF BEES

for Mary Ann Bentler

The summer you went to Anatone
She was twenty-six, divorced.
Her farmhouse stood proud
On flatland. Heat swelled up
From the buckling soil, rotted
The thin slat steps to wheeze
Dry as the rasp of sleepers.
You watched the sun,
The dry moon that hung thin
As smoke-dust kicked to sky
From cattle
Plodding
To fences
Looking
For wind.
Mornings you'd wake to heat calling
Like a dream, her father frying
Flapjacks, the slather-foam mouths
Of thirsty cattle sucking
Wind. Weeds whispered dry
As the voices of old women.
Told you this home would claim your first
                    Then the hard rocks
                              Then the dust-dry soil
                                        Then wind.
And you knew too, when you watched her herding
Cattle, you belonged
To old barns, chicken coops,
Sun-dusted fields where wind
Was a clean horizon.

She'd saddle up the field horse for you,
The one that cut fast toward strays,
Ran to the least touch of rein.
You rode stiff in the saddle

Afraid of hard rocks,
Hard ground,
Hard knocks.
You didn't see the morning lark shoot up
From grass until you fell toward sleep,
Those old dreams that say this life is
More real when you let go. Bees
Hummed a clear-death venom hotter
Than the lather-smooth back of your horse running
Home. You ran too, pulling
Bees from your wind-tangled hair. And the wind of your passing
Hummed with the sound of more bees. With each breath
Your swelling tongue renamed them:
Maybe black bees,
Maybe bumblebees,
Then again, yellow jackets
Then again, hornets,
Then again black bees, then again
And again, swallowing names of bees.
Their memory became colorless, distant as the waving horizon
Scorched by sun. Bees sizzled the small of your back,
Called back your steps to remember:
Your mother had an allergy to bees,
Swelled up cadaver-dark one summer,
Told fever stories. Each summer after
She stood in the kitchen looking toward fields
Buzzing with clover. On her neck, the backs of her legs,
Thin blue veins were a map to memory.
Fever stories:
Grampa, dead ten years, was smiling,
She said, holding her hand.
And the young girl who laughed
Like you, ("You remember her dear.") lost
To the irrigation ditch in '58.
She came back too,
Back to your mother's bedside,
Back to laugh at death. And when your mother said,

"She's laughing, listen dear."
You closed your eyes,
Remembered only burial dirt, her small grave sinking
To years,
And always thereafter,
Her dry, dry mouth open
Hot with the memory of bees.

Your friend came from nowhere,
Pulled your shirt off,
Screamed a cloud of bees toward heaven,
Slapped bees with both hands,
Slapped your back
            your stomach
            your breasts.
When the neighbor drove by,
She rolled her window
Tight to bees.
Slow dust salve billowed
The trial of her car, followed
Her like a bad memory.

That night your friend sat close to you,
Told you stories of other times:
Summer of hummingbirds,
Summer of rattlers,
Summer of rain and of wind,
Each with a voice of its own,
Always calling,
        The creak of a summer screen door,
         A car turns off the highway lighting
          A pale dust road going
           Home. Your mother waving,
            The drowned girl laughing,
             The high buzzing wires,
              The dry-dust soil,
               Then wind.

ANITA ENDREZZE

Anita Endrezze is a well-known Yaqui artist and writer. Raised in California, Hawaii, Washington, and Oregon, she now makes her home in Spokane, Washington. She earned her M.A. in Creative Writing from Eastern Washington University in 1975.

She has published poems and stories in a number of magazines and books including *Voices of the Rainbow* (Viking Press), *Carriers of the Dream Wheel*, *Harper's Anthology of 20th Century Native American Poetry* (both on Harper & Row), and *Songs of This Earth on Turtle's Back* (Greenfield Review Press).

In 1983 she published two chapbooks: *Burning the Fields* (Confluence Press) and *The North Country* (Blue Clouds Press).

Anita's artwork has been used to illustrate a number of books on American Indian writing. She has illustrated the cover of *Harper's Anthology of 20th Century Native American Poetry* (Harper & Row, 1988) and most recently one of her paintings was chosen for the cover of a special American Indian issue of *The Wooster Review*.

Anita is currently working on a collection of short stories that combine straightforward narratives tinged with "the thread of dreams" and stories told from the point of view of the "Dream-Walker." Anita's writing celebrates the "eternal feminine energy" and tries to "balance the 'dreaminess of the spiritual' with the harder lines of plot and language."

THE DIETER'S DAUGHTER

Mom's got this taco guy's poem
taped to the fridge, some ode to celery,
which she is always eating.
The celery, I mean, not the poem
which talks about green angels
and fragile corsets. I don't get it,
but Mom says by the time she reads it
she forgets she's hungry. One stalk
for breakfast, along with half a grapefruit,
or a glass of aloe vera juice,
you know that stuff that comes from cactus,
and one stalk for lunch
with some protein drink
that tastes like dried placenta,
did you know that they put cow placenta
in make-up, face cream, stuff like that?
Yuck. Well, Mom says it's never too early
to wish you looked different,
which means I got to eat that crap too.
Mom says: your body is a temple,
not the place all good twinkies go to.
Mom says: that boys remember
girls that're slender.
Mom says that underneath all this fat
there's a whole new me,
one I'd really like if only I gave myself
the chance. Mom says: you are
what you eat, which is why she eats celery,
because she wants to be thin,
not green or stringy, of course—
am I talking too fast?—
but thin as paper
like the hearts we cut out
and send to ourselves,
don't tell anyone,

like the hearts of gold
melons we eat
down
to the bitter rind.

I WAS BORN

I was born
    husk of jelly-
fish
    afterbirth
like a blood-orange

I was born
    in a storm
the rain white as milk
  small priestess of sand-
waves   sea-rust   salt grass

I was born
  above Las Coyotes Blvd
where there are no coyotes
  and not far from the river
which had no water
  and near orange groves
that grew houses all alike

I was born
with a leg like a crook
  it always ran away from Right
until it was cast
  in a shell
and grew alike
so I could walk with everyone's stride

But because I was born
  in storm's eye

I could see yerba buena
   in the milk
waves of poppies
   yellowing in the dry wind
and lunar horses
   trembling in the bamboo

in short   I was born
in a body
that renews the soul

I was born little
palm heart
little
shadow
of a greater one

THE LIGHT THAT PASSES

the light that passes through stones
is the same light that reddens the apples

the light that lingers to green
the wheat is the same that whitens
the insides of chestnuts

the light that is the coronation
of my hair is the same light
that gloves your hands

the mouth that is the wolf of the North Wind
is the same mouth that blackens
the blossom

the mouth that is the voice
of floods is the same that consents
to the joining of clay and sun

the mouth that is the companion
to sunflowers of honey is the same
that kisses you

the eyes that see stemfuls of light
are the same that see the matriarchs
dancing in mountains

the eyes that see warships in skeletons
are the same that see stars in eggshells

the eyes that see you walking in the grass
when there's nothing but the wind
are the same eyes that see
distance sealing a great door

OCTOBER MORNING WALK

for Aaron

On the pond, frost floats like rice paper,
cattails exclaiming the absence of mallards.
Between frost and water, drowned wasps
promise the water its one dream: to fly.
Algae begins its elegy, lamenting summer.
Aaron, circling the pond, kicks the thistles
whose ragged heads are in a final drowse.
Over us, the last sharp-shinned hawk
robs the air of its patented horizon.
In this cold, I hunger for a field of suns
while my son day-dreams about a moon
as white as a feather and an owl
whose eyes are icy moons in an empty sky.
Aaron is Autumn's child. I follow him
into the dark-tufted meadow where frost's
fragile language sparkles on his tongue.

THE MAP-MAKER'S DAUGHTER

the geography of love is terra infirma

it is a paper boat
navigated by mates
with stars in their eyes
cartographers of the fiery unknown

it is the woman's sure hand
at the helm of twilight, the salt
compass of her desire

* * * *

the map of longing is at the edge
of two distant bodies

it is the rain that launches thirst

it is the palm leaf floating on waters
far from shore

* * * *

the secret passage into the interior
is in my intemperate estuary

the sweet and languorous flowering
is in the caliber of your hands

* * * *

the circular motion of our journeying
is the radius of sky and sea, deep
territories we name
after ourselves

MAXINE FRANKLIN

"I've always loved walking, reading, and writing, these being the most satisfying spiritual exercises to me. I'm Athabascan and Eskimo with a few genes contributed by Europeans. My writing comes from my relationship with the earth, and my sense of geologic time, most expressed in the red-rock canyon country of the American Southwest, my favorite of all places. During my college days, working for my degrees in biology and dental hygiene, I spent several wonderful summers on fire lookouts in North Cascades National Park. Presently working and residing in Anchorage, I would love to go back to college for an MFA in creative writing."

SKAGIT RIVER SPIRITS

We can say this of our house:
We live somewhere beyond it.
The river flows through us, endless and quiet
Except at flood time. The moon rises
Outside our windows. We live there too,
Dwell in flood and moonrise.
We float on a skin of light, slipping
Silver shapes and shadows.
We that are nothing grant only spaces.

[Untitled]

Fields roll away
Brown corn, brown furrows
Full of shadows, curving.
The sun, squash-colored as it goes down.
I drive north to Sioux Falls.
Trust its there. Think on beauty.
The sky hovers, pale and wintry.

An amber dog lies
His head among dried grass by the road.
In eternity, you might say. The grass
Waves, brittle. I drive on . . .

A deer there in gentle
Curve of country beside the highway—
Large-bellied, legs folded
No way they ever turned in life.
I turn the radio on and hear
Aaron Copeland's "For Our Town."

Now evening. Cattle
Carried in huge trucks, speed by,
Drugged and hopeless, bound for glory.

I think of Christ and all sacrifices—
How mismanaged they all are.

The sky lies open like a melon or shaded
Shell. Brown earth below, in shadow now,
Carved for the platter. Cold lights
Wink up from distant farms. We slide
So easy away from the light.

THE MAN WHO SHOT RAVENS: THREE VIEWS

1. *The Villagers'*
The teacher came to our village.
My mother told me this.
She, and all the other children, were afraid
But didn't know why. Then, one day
He took his gun
And shot Ravens
By the river.

"O-o-o-h, he should not have done that.
Something terrible will happen to him!"
They all whispered, like an omen,
Or a spell. "That man's crazy!"

2. *The Man's*
My God . . .
                the winters
Last forever!
The yellow dog-pissed
Snow, the piles of bones
The smell of blood
Animal, and menstrual
The wind
The superstitious calm
The waiting, the mockery
Of dark eyes. The circle closed

Beyond my life. I have
No face here. Their name for me:
"Empty Pot"
                    And those ravens—
They bode evil
Their dark forbearance
Their negation
Faces of the devil!
My God, . . . Why hast thou forsaken. . . ?

3. *The Ravens'*
An explosion of sound
Shrinks the distance. One of us
Suddenly a tumbling
Fall of feathers. Head arcs to spine,
Eyes toward the wind. The snow
Stains red, a small momentary
Fountain. Feathers glint in the hard light.
Flecks of light—all colors—scattered
Wide on the residual wind. The man
Steps into our shadow as he turns away.

4. *Afterword*
"Sure enough" said my mother
"His wife got T.B. and died. His second
wife died too, I don't know what of. He himself
Almost died, a burst appendix in the dead of winter.
They took him out one night by dogsled, unconscious
And moaning. He came back months later, a walking
Skeleton. . . . All because he shot those Ravens
By the river, a long time ago."

WYOMING REMEMBERED

At evening
All is changed
The scent of sage
Boils up like a gentle
Campfire stew
Tendrils of aroma
Drift over time
And great distance
Sky fires up
Streamers of lit clouds
All flying plumes of purple
Tweed sagebrush flats breathe
Dark pools from every shallow
Hollow. A flame of cloud
Flares and fades
I bite into peppergrass
Gather my fire

PHIL GEORGE

Born in Seattle, Washington in 1946, Phil George calls the Puget Sound home. He is Wallowa Nez Perce and Alaskan Tsimshian.

A champion Traditional Plateau dancer, he designs and makes his own outfits. He has been a Cub Scout, a Boy Scout, Vietnam veteran, and Congressional Intern in the U.S. House of Representatives in Washington, D.C. He toured with the Native American Theater Ensemble out of New York City and travels the country giving writing workshops upon request. He performs some of his poetry in sign language dressed in a white buffalo headdress and white buckskin regalia.

Phil George's work has appeared in several anthologies. Vincent Price read his work on the Dick Cavett Show and the Johnny Carson Show; the late Senator Frank Church read his poetry before Congress when Phil won a Gold Medal for National Poetry Day. He has read his poetry for Radio Free Europe and it was translated into several languages. Phil's poetry also received much acclaim at the Yugoslavian sponsored "Native American Writers' Festival."

Kautsas (Grandmothers), his first chapbook, is sold exclusively at the Nez Perce National Historical Park in Spaulding, Idaho. There his poetry enhances museum cases and walls. Phil also wrote, produced, and narrated "A Season of Grandmothers" for PBS.

AN-HIMH HI-HI (WHITE WINTER)

From the dark, far, north, white in snow,
Cold Maker comes prancing: White as snow.
Thunder Birds flap loud, enormous wings as
Pink Eyes sings icy songs, Spear Pointing—
Bizarre, breath-blowing—Blizzard Songs.

All white: From the ice-crusted fetlocks above the
White striped hooves of his albino Appaloosa to
White braids, silver as this silent moon;
White trailed warbonnet flowing to
White mountain goat foot-furs;
White buckskins fringed in
White flowing ermines;
White buffalo saddle,
White stone spear,
White owl fan,
White man,
White
* * *
*

Snow Maker demands Winter's preparation!
Cold Maker commands Winter's hibernation—
Safe circle within Hearth's warm harmony . . .
From the far, dark, north, white in snow . . .
Cold Maker comes prancing: White as snow . . .

GRAND ENTRY

New York, Red Lake, Santa Fe,
Anadarko and Arlee along the way—
Pickup campers, weary hitchhikers,
Motor homes, vans, and bikers.

Wickiups, wigwams, tepees new,
Adobe pueblos and hogans, too!
Pageants, rodeos, stick-game teams,
Skinjins strutting in cowboy jeans.

Rugged fun not for the frail;
Never-ending pow-wow trail!
$1,000 pot to stop on a dime;
Suburbia, acculturated "49"!

Spinning shawls and bustled prancers
Those jet setting tribal dancers.
'Fresh off the rez' and genteel gentry
Sure won't miss this fine Grand Entry . . . .

Behind Feather Flags veterans lead;
A long Honor Song is what we need.
Come enter our circle elegant and proud . . . .
In awesome silence stands the crowd . . . .

When your Last Morning Sky opens just for you
Everyone shall stand as you dance on through . . . .

NORTHWEST NATIVES: WHERE HAVE ALL OUR PEOPLE GONE?

Homicide, infanticide, genocide, ethnocide: Satsop, Clatsop, Samish, Sammamish, Sahewamish, Swinomish, Semiahmoos, Shimishmoos, Shoshone, Shasta, Shyiks, Skagit, Skalakhans, Spokanes, Sinkiuses, Sinkaietks, Skitwishes, Skalizises, Siletzes, Seapcats.

Where have all our people gone? Skokumchucks, Skokomish, Skokimish, Skopahmish, Skykomish, Squinomish, Suquamish, Squawmish, Squaxin, Snohomish, Snoqualmie, Stillaguamish, Duamish, Stakamish, Stillacoom, Skiloot, Sanpoil, San Juans, and Hohs?

Where have all our People gone? Entiat, Tenino, Tututnis, Naltunnetunne, Twana, Tyighes, Tukspush, Tiatnapums, Ahalpams, Pushwannapams, Wanapams, Wisscopams, Wenatschapams, Wahkiakums, Hoquiams, Chimacums, Wascos, Wishram, Washam, Wyam, Whiskahs, Makahs, Micals, Wadatokas, Wheelappas, Willaps, Swalla, Wallowas, Watlalas, Mollalas, Clowwewallas, Walla Wallas, Willamettes, Umatillas, Yoncallas, Yaquinas, Yakimas, Wauykmas, Yamels, Woocksockwillacums, Tillamooks, Tonaskets, and Togotokases?

Where have all our People gone? Hulhwaluqs, Hanchiukes, Hanshokes, Kwalhioquas, Okanagons, Quileutes, Quilceeds, Quintiousas, Queets, Kikialluses, Palouses, Cayuses, Chualpays, Calapooyas, Kahmiltpahs, and Kwalhioquas?

Where have all Our People gone? Boises, Banoocks, Chinooks, Chilliwacks, Chilliwists, Ochechotes, Chewelahs, Chehalises, Chelans, Chelamelas, Cathlamets, Klamaths, Clackamases, Clahnaquahs, Klinquits, Clallams, Coeur D'Alenes, Coquilles, Colvilles, Cowlitz, Cowichans, Kawachens, Kowwassayee, Kolsids, Kartars, Kalispels, Konkonelps, Kootenais, Kittitas, Klickitats, Konnaacks, Nooksacks, Nitnats, Nootkas, Nasomahs, Nuwahas, Nesquallys, Nehalems, Nespelems, Nekelims, Nez Perce, Popskillows, Pisquows, Pailsks, Puyallups, Skinpahs, Peniyahs, and Ozettes?

Where have all Our People gone? Alsea, Clatskanie, Chilluckittequaw, Miwaletas, Metcowwees, Multnomahs, Muckleshoots, Modocs, Warm Springs, Duhlelips, Tulalips, Humptulips, Liaywas, Lummi, and Lemhi?

WHERE HAVE ALL OUR PEOPLE GONE? Disease decimation, assassination, extermination, annihilation, massacre, murder, butcher, slaughter—
Oh where has the eagle gone?

THUMBING GUY

If it fits in his pack he'll tote it along—
Jogging cadence stick game song . . . .
Loud as he can just like a Marine!
Early morning, lonely terrain.

Back roads route, country folk—
Dips at the bridge, enjoys a smoke—
Soaks his shirt, cools down a bit—
Down the road is easy sweat . . . .

Mirror shades, big brim black hat
Knows those songs that Pow-wow Cat!
Thumbing Guy's a gambler, too,
Bone tosser through and through . . . .

Here comes a rig— 'A One-eye Ford!'
Mufflers loose, engines roared;
Goin' all night right light still on!
Headed down to Tepee Town . . . .

Carload of Skins almost awake;
Need new driver—goodness sake!
Cheek over man he'll take that wheel
To the Circle—What a deal!

So when you spy a Thumbing Guy
With warpaint on don't pass him by!
Pick him up 'cuz he's good luck!
He'll skindian charm your pow-wow truck.

He's a winner he's for real;
Coyote sniffing his next meal!
Has always been along these trails—
Seek him find him—never fails!

ICE FISHIN'

Ice fishin' is our mission
Up on Owhi Lake—
We get to eat, nature's treat
With fry bread Ma will make!

Sure exciting fish all biting
On the worm and corn—
Pulling out, speckled trout
Before the coming storm.

Raven cries in turquoise skies,
Ascending silver moon—
Long blue shadows, along cold meadows
We've got to be leaving soon . . . .

* * * *

Grab yer skillet, time to fill it
With spuds and other things!
The pan is greased, we're gonna feast!
On food fit for kings!

Caught that whopper for our supper,
Didn't think that I was able;
I don't know why you'd be so shy
Eating at this table!

For a moment, a prayer won't it
Seem only fair?
To give thanks for the dish, all these fish,
Showing we really care?

And so scarf up, yer hungry pup
Gets 'Friskies' tonight!
I can hardly wait, to dig more bait,
And give those fish a fight!

JANET CAMPBELL HALE

Janet Campbell Hale is a member of the Coeur D'Alene Tribe of northern Idaho. She graduated from the University of California, Berkeley, in 1974, then studied law also at Berkeley for two years, and earned her M.A. in English from the University of California, Davis, in 1984. She has taught language and literature courses at Berkeley, Davis, Western Washington University in Bellingham, and Lummi Community College, also in Bellingham. She was Writer-in-Residence at the University of Washington (1985–86) and has taught at the University of Oregon (Spring 1987) and at the Centrum Foundation, Port Townsend, Washington (Summer 1987).

Her books include *The Owl's Song*, a novel (1974); *Custer Lives in Humboldt County*, a collection of poetry (1977); and *The Jailing of Cecilia Capture*, a novel (1985). *The Jailing of Cecilia Capture* was nominated for six literary awards including the Pulitzer Prize.

Ms. Hale currently lives in New York City, where she is writing a historical novel.

ANCESTRESS

I am brown-skinned orphaned sister,
Child only of the never-known long dead,
Child only of they
Who walk with me in the cold damp
Beside the sea.
(See how the great dark mountains make us shelter)
Indian grandmothers of the long ago,
How much sweeter could the old days have been
Than these belonging to me now?

They cannot whisper lies
Whom I have called forth and cannot harm,
Can only say what I would have them say:
"Yes, Grandchild, you who are *from* us
Are *of* us too." Yes.
Hear the beat of the Indian drums.
See the eagle how it circles, circles.

When I myself
Return to earth and sky and sea
And no one lives who remembers me,
Then I will be at the side of she who imagines me there,
Her old Indian ancestress.
I lived here once (she will have me say)
And like yourself walked along these shores
And breathed the salt-air
And felt the wind on my face.
Just like you, granddaughter's granddaughter.
Through you we endure,
We spirits of the long-dead
Who cannot whisper lies,
Who cannot turn away,
Who can only love
And say yes, it was as you say.
Look to the great dark mountains,
Blood of my blood.

Hear the drums . . . drums . . . drums.
See there the eagle how it glides,
How it circles, circles.

Autobiography in Fiction

My mother and older sisters used to like to tell a story about how I thought I was writing a book the winter I turned four years old. I would write like this: line after line, page after page until I had filled three Big Chief Tablets.

Sometimes they would ask me to read from my work and I would read something like this, "The little girl was sitting quietly at the kitchen table writing. Just then her big sister came into the room and asked her to read something of what she had written to her."

I was compulsive about it, they said. I had to write in my tablets every day.

I can still, in a fragmented way, remember that awful winter. My mother had taken me and my two teen-aged sisters (the oldest one was married) and left my father, who was away from home at the time on "a bender." She had no resources, though, and no place to run to. We went to Medical Lake, Washington, and lived with my mother's sister and her family. It was cold and we were isolated in the country and it seemed like a blizzard went on constantly. In my memories of that winter it was always blizzarding.

I can remember writing in those tablets, too, though I can't remember what I wrote. I remember opening myself up and focusing all my energy, channeling it into the "writing." I didn't understand then what writing was, that letters represented different sounds and put together they made words which were symbols that stood for thoughts and feelings and objects in the physical world.

In my four-year-old's mind I believed reading and writing worked more or less like this:

The writer, when she makes the marks upon the paper, must concentrate very very hard, must put everything she has into this making of marks, must think the thoughts and feel the feelings deeply and intensely because it would be through this intensity that the thoughts of the writer would be transferred from the writer's mind onto the paper. Then, if the writer had managed to leave her emotions and thoughts in the marks on the paper, a reader could come along and pick up the paper and look at these marks and the reader could feel and think as the writer had when the writer wrote on the pages. The thoughts and feelings would remain as long as the marks remained on the paper, or as long as the paper would last.

I think that that was not very different from the way I would write later on, after I had learned to read and write in the conventional sense, as a teenager expressing myself in poetry no one would ever read and much later as an adult, writer of novels. If it is to be real and true, if you are to write the deep truth down and have it understood the way you intend, then you must concentrate all your energy, must throw off pretensions and bare your soul, write with the utmost sincerity and intensity whatever it is you want to say, right down to your very core.

I don't remember what it was I wrote about that winter at Medical Lake when I filled three Big Chief Tablets with writing. I like to think it was something more than reportage, though, that I was in some way interpreting life, giving some order to the chaos my life had become, and in this writing was keeping my own counsel.

The More Or Less Autobiographical Story I Will Write From My Sick Bed at St. Luke's Hospital

A friend has brought me a notebook and a pen and I am to write a story. If it turns out I can't write a story after all, or if I do but it isn't any good . . . that will be okay because I am lying in my sick bed. I am in fact really doing this for therapeutic, not artistic reasons.

My story will be, of course, autobiographical, more or less . . . in a manner of speaking, and after it gets famous people will ask me if it is. And I'll think "how tiresome" and try to think of something literary to say, knowing it really won't matter what I say.

Something literary like "Not autobiographical in a literal sense, but I suppose it is the same way that everything one writes is in some way based on his or her own personal vision of life. But fiction is concerned with a higher truth."

It won't matter what I say because most people want to believe that it is, indeed, the author's own life that is displayed in such naked, intimate, detail to public view. I, as a writer, will have been concerned with the verisimilitude of the story, will have taken pains to make my characters and their situations seem real (and to accomplish this end I do things like have one protagonist go to law school, have another live on the Northwest Coast—not because I want to write about myself but because I know through personal experience what it is like to be in law school. I know what it feels like to live in a place where I am awakened by the sound of the surf, and it rains most all of the time, and dramatic, snow-capped mountains are a daily presence. Interviewers often remark on how my characters' lives "parallel" my own despite the claim that what I write is not autobiography. Yet, really, it is by sharing my own experiences with my fictional characters I am able to breathe life and authenticity into them).

One plot-developing exercise I assign my creative writing students is to bring in short news stories from a daily paper, and then, from the bare bones of such a story to develop a plot, then flesh it out into a story.

Someone will always remind me, "But you said we write from our own experience," as though such a statement were contradictory to the assignment.

I say, "None of us knows how anyone else perceives the world, what another person feels or thinks. We only know what we ourselves feel and think and what others tell us of their experience. In fiction we create the illusion that we can know what someone else knows and feels. We attempt to share our experience with others through our work.

Suppose you have a character in your story walk down the road and you describe his feelings as he does this. The feel of a light rain on his face, the gravel under his shoes, the sound of a car engine in the distance. See, you really only know those things from your own experience . . . how the gravel feels beneath your shoes as you walk over it. You give your experience to your characters. That does not mean, however, that he is you."

My story, I think, will be about a woman who, like me, was born in 1946. As the story opens, in late 1986, she has been through almost a year of mourning for her lost youth. She wants to stop mourning, to settle into middle-age.

Then you won't have to worry about gray hair or crow's feet, not being noticed (*really* noticed) anymore by men. Then you won't care so much because you will have arrived at a new area in your life . . . you'll be "accepting"—you'll settle in—you won't bark or whine or wish it weren't true. You'll just *be* middle-aged.

So let's give this forty-year-old woman a name. Julia is fine. And a life. A life, sort of, more or less, like my own.

She is, like me, a writer, and this is the first year she has ever tried to live as a full-time writer, to not have any other kind of employment. She has only recently begun to realize the seriousness of her work . . . that is, that it is through her work that she keeps herself together. Through her work she struggles to define herself and her reality. Like me, she lives alone and is divorced. But I have two children while she has none.

She lives in a small, old town on the Washington coast. Maybe Bellingham. Maybe not. Maybe a meshing of Bellingham and Neah Bay with a dash of Port Townsend thrown in.

Her town will be, like Bellingham, a commercial fisherman's town. (Port Townsend is much too trendy.) Georgia-Pacific paper mill is a nice touch, I think, very smelly and we know by its presence that this is a working-class town. Yet Bellingham also contains a large enclave of yuppies and that is not the way I want her town to be.

I want her to feel as I feel at Neah Bay,* at earth's end. (You see the metaphor, don't you? She is at her own earth's end—no husband or prospect of one. No lover. No children, approaching the end of her childbearing years. And though her work has enjoyed some critical attention, she, unlike myself, has not published with major presses, has not received award nominations and wide critical acclaim. The year she had decided to spend writing is a "this is it—it's now or never" sort of thing.)

*Neah Bay, home of the Makah Indians, is a village at the old site of Ozette, at the tip of the Olympic Peninsula, as far north and west you can get and still be in the continental United States.

Land's End may be the name of her town. Or Earth's End also like the isolation of Neah Bay, how mud slides make the road impassable during the winter and I like the way sea lions loll casually about on the rocks there and I would like to have them in my story.

The house she lives in is a hundred years old, is musty-smelling and poorly insulated. It belongs to Julia's friend whom she first knew when they were thirteen years old at boarding school. Let's call her friend "Mona."

Mona's aunt died in the house several months before Mona told Julia she could come live there.

It once belonged to Mona's grandparents and Mona visited there often as a child.

Mona comes to the house to pack away her aunt's belongings in the first days that Julia is there. Mona needs Julia's company as she sorts through the old woman's things. She needs to tell an interested, sympathetic person about her aunt's life and some of her own memories connected with the house.

Mona tells her, by the way, there are a good many snakes around here—all over lurking in the overgrown grass . . . those ugly, black kind you see around these parts, sometimes with yellow stripes running down their backs.

Once, Mona tells her, when she was a little girl, she came upon a startling sight in the back yard: a mother snake with her brood of squirming, writhing, intertwining baby snakes.

Julia resolves to never go in the backyard. She won't even go out there to hang laundry on the line. She wonders if a man would allow himself to be intimidated by snakes, or if he would be afraid but not admit that he was out of a need to preserve his macho self-image.

Julia may only live in the house until the estate is probated. Maybe it will be six or seven months. No longer than nine months.

Julia sets up her desk by the window in the living room and arranges her writing materials. She writes letters to people and tells them of her "studio", how the window in front of the desk overlooks the bay and she watches the fishing boats going out and coming in . . . and the occasional tall ship. She walks on the beach every day as a proper writer would. Now I am a real writer, she tells herself, no longer an overworked social worker trying to sneak in an hour's writing time here and there.

Julia also has a drinking problem. I don't think I will go into it much, beyond just letting the reader know that it is connected to Julia's melancholy and she is afraid of it taking her over as it took over her brother after his return from Vietnam.

When Julia was in Seattle, still working at her social worker's job, she wrote Mona a letter about her need for peace, how she wanted to write but had neither time nor energy after her grueling day's work at Child Protective Services.

About the drinking she wrote: "It isn't a matter, anymore, of it being an embarrassment, of feeling like I am a weak person for using it to help me make it through the night. I wish that that were all it was.

"It's much more now. It's as though I leave myself each time I drink and something evil takes hold. I'm not talking about Dr. Jekyll and Mr. Hyde stuff. I don't mean that I do wicked, damaging things, that I steal or hurt or kill or anything. I mean it feels like *I* am what the alcohol wants. Me. And each time I leave myself the evil grows stronger. I have to not drink. I've got to. Somehow I must stop or, like Doc Holliday at the OK Corral, I will have to prepare to forfeit my soul."

Mona, who is her oldest friend, wrote her a letter the same day she received Julia's letter and said, "Come here. Live in the old house for awhile. Write. Search for a better job. Catch your breath." Julia now has begun a novel which is progressing well. She hasn't had a drink in six months.

A distancing process has occurred. I have become Julia. I can see her and she is not me.

Though she is my age she is older-looking than I, and plainer than I am (or at least than I imagine myself to be). I am taller than average. Quite tall, in fact, but I don't want her to be. She is just average height. Rather dumpy-looking.

She has heavy hips and thighs, large feet. She has short arms and a rather frail upper body, narrow shoulders and ribcage. Large breasts.

I imagine Julia examining her breasts in the mirror. How they have changed since her youth, she thinks. Is it noticeable when she is dressed how they have changed? Do people who see her walking along the street assume she has middle-aged breasts, no longer plump and bouncy beneath her bra, turtleneck, sweatshirt?

She wears a red cotton bandana over her dark hair, tied behind at the nape of her neck. Her hair has begun to turn gray. She will not dye it because long ago she promised herself she would never be so vain as to dye her hair.

I see her as a rather ruddy-complexioned (Irish skin, women with that kind of skin like to say). The kind of woman who can't walk on the beach for long when the sun is out and who must keep moving her position outdoors to follow the shade because her skin is too sensitive to sunlight.

Either I will make no mention of her race or she is just a white-looking Indian. I don't think race will be an issue . . . or maybe it will. Two marriages. One abortion. No children.

For years Julia owned a big black St. Bernard/Labrador named Bjorn whom she loved, who died, whom she misses.

She dreams about Bjorn. She wishes he were there to walk on the beach with her, to lie at her feet while she reads or writes, to reach down and touch.

Stories aren't written as a series of intellectual decisions. It is an intuitive sort of thing.

The intellect controls, selects, and rejects, yet the story doesn't come from the intellect. It is brewed in the unconscious—fiction comes from the deeper, darker places in the writer's soul, the same places that dreams come from, and, as in the making of dreams, the unconscious makes use of bits and pieces as it weaves its fiction tapestry: autobiography, yes, if there is anything there that can be used, and other people's works, both fiction and fact, all that you experience.

Fiction speaks in symbolic language, symbols both personal and universal. Fiction and dreams spring from a common well. Dreams, though, speak to the individual—draw attention to suppressed needs, answer troublesome questions, make clear to the dreamer that which was clouded.

In the practice of fiction artists speak not only to the self but to others as well. Fiction illuminates, imposes order where there was none. Where autobiography, so-called, is used as a basis for fiction, a rearrangement, a transformation must occur.

I first became aware of how compelling this "rearrangement" is in my writing when someone from the University of Nebraska Press wrote me and asked me to submit a short autobiography for inclusion in an anthology of writer's autobiographies.

I began writing what intended to be an honest, sincere, real story about my life.

Before I knew it I was writing about Carmen Miranda and how when I was a little girl I'd wanted to grow up to be just like her and I had Carmen Miranda paper dolls and coloring books and used to fantasize about Carmen Miranda being my real mother . . . that one day she would come to reclaim me and I'd drawn a picture of Carmen and myself embracing and wrote a caption "Mother and Daughter Reunited" and tacked it to the wall above my little bed.

I was aware of lying, yet I couldn't stop myself, no . . . I didn't care to stop myself. All this stuff about Carmen Miranda was a lie. I'd liked her quite a lot but that was all. (And if it had been the way I wrote about it I doubt that I would have wanted to tell anyone about it, let alone state it in writing for publication. I am not willing, as most people aren't, to expose my real private life for contemplation.)

And the real life drawing was this: when my daughter was about ten she was to leave me to go spend the summer with her father. This would be our first long separation and I was feeling sad and knew how deeply I would miss her.

She drew a picture of the two of us embracing, wrote the caption "Mother and Daughter Reunited" and taped it to the wall. This was for me to look at when I got lonesome so that I could remind myself that she would be coming back.

So there are elements of truth in the passage about Carmen Miranda but the passage was not the truth. And I didn't know why I was writing those things but I went on with it anyway.

When I finished and read it over I saw immediately that this was really the material I needed to go into the novel I was then writing, *The Jailing of Cecilia Capture*.

If it were autobiography the whole passage would be a pack of lies. But it was not autobiography at all, but fiction, you see. I used it in my novel and decided against writing an autobiography for the University of Nebraska anthology.

I don't get an idea for a story and then set about writing the story. I've got to let the story have its own way. I see myself, then, as the servant of my fiction rather than me using my fiction as a vehicle to convey my predetermined "message."

For instance: when I was in intensive care, watching my heart beat thump its way across the screen, I thought, as I think many people do in similar circumstances, about my own mortality, about how fleeting life is. I thought of all the things I haven't done yet, how much I still wanted to do and see. I thought of patching up differences. If I ever get out of here, I thought, I will be different. I thought of how I would like to write a story in which I would share my new insights with others.

I would like to write a story like this: a forty-year-old woman, when she is seriously ill, suddenly understands how she hadn't been living life to the fullest. She resolves that when she gets out of the hospital she is going to do all these good works: visit old peoples homes, donate money to orphanages, call old friends she has been neglecting for a long time. Maybe she will attempt to reconcile with a sister or other relative from whom she has been estranged for years. But she can't do any of these things because she dies in the hospital. Then the story would be about life before it's too late. Or maybe she gets well and gets out of the hospital and forgets how she felt in her time of crisis and goes back to being ordinary and selfish.

I knew, though, even as I imagined such a story, that it would never see the light of day because it had no life of its own.

Although acquiring a deep appreciation of life and wanting to live life for all it was worth was a deeply meaningful experience on a personal level, it was not the stuff stories are made of. It would be a mere contrivance. I would have to fashion a story to convince my reader of my point of view. I would have to attempt to manipulate the emotions of my reader and this is not the way honest fiction is written.

Getting back to my Julia in her creaky old house at Earth's End: I will have to work with her, let her story emerge. Thus the vague, intangible gnawing feelings, the haunting images are allowed to see the light of day, are given form, are brought into tangible existence.

This is how writers articulate their own vision and create a means through which that vision can be shared with other people.

Not so simple then as "autobiography" is it. Real life comes into play only insofar as it can serve the purpose of art.

An old woman has been admitted to the room across the hall. She is very old, very thin and fragile-looking. I keep getting up and closing the door so I won't have to see her as she lies in bed in her darkened room in the light from the TV screen because the sight is so disturbing to me. The nurses keep reopening the door. The old woman wears a lime-green crocheted cap.

The image of the frail old woman in a green cap staring at TV haunts me, even in my sleep. She is always alone. No one ever visits. Maybe she will find her way into my fiction one day. Maybe not. Making fiction is a mysterious process.

ROGER JACK

Roger Jack is a member of the Confederated Tribes of the Colville Indian Reservation. He was born and raised in Nespelem, Washington. His educational degrees include an Associate of Fine Arts degree in Creative Writing from the Institute of American Indian Arts in Santa Fe, New Mexico; he has earned Bachelor of Arts degrees in English and Education as well as a Master of Fine Arts in Creative Writing from Eastern Washington University in Cheney, Washington. In fall of 1988 he began work in the Ph.D. program in American Studies at Washington State University in Pullman, Washington.

Roger writes that his people and his culture are the "sustenance of my education—and the essence of my writing." His work has been published in many journals and anthologies including *New York Quarterly*, *Spawning the Medicine River*, *Earth Power Coming*, and *The Clouds Threw This Light*. He has also written a one-act play, *Buckskin Curtains*.

An Indian Story

Aunt Greta was always a slow person. Grandpa used to say she was like an old lady out of the old days who never hurried herself for anything, no matter what. She was only forty-five, heavyset, dark-complexioned, and very knowledgeable of the old ways, which made her seem even older. Most of the time she wore her hair straight up or in a ponytail that hung below her beltline. At home she wore pants and big, baggy shirts, but at tribal gatherings she wore her light blue calico dress, beaded moccasins, hair braided and clasped with beaded barrettes. Sometimes she wore a scarf on her head like ladies older than she. She said we emulate those we love and care for. I liked seeing her dressed for ceremonials. Even more, I liked seeing her stand before crowds of tribal members and guests translating the old language to the new for our elders, or speaking on behalf of the younger people who had no understanding of the Indian language. It made me proud to be her nephew and her son.

My mom died when I was little. Dad took care of me as best he could after that. He worked hard and earned good money as an accountant at the agency. But about a year after Mom died he married a half-breed Indian and this made me feel very uncomfortable. Besides, she had a child of her own who was white. We fought a lot —me and Jeffrey Pine—and then I'd get into trouble because I was older and was supposed to know better than to misbehave.

I ran away from home one day when everyone was gone—actually, I walked to Aunt Greta's and asked if I could move in with her since I had already spent so much time with her anyway. Then after I had gone to bed that night, Dad came looking for me and Aunt Greta told him what I had told her about my wanting to move in with her. He said it would be all right for awhile, then we would decide what to do about it later. That was a long time ago. Now I am out of high school and going to college. Meanwhile, Jeffrey Pine is a high-school drop out and living with the folks.

Aunt Greta was married a long time ago. She married a guy named Mathew who made her very happy. They never had children, but when persistent people asked either of them what was wrong, they would simply reply they were working on it. Then Mathew died during their fifth year of marriage. No children. No legacy. After that Aunt Greta took care of Grandpa, who had moved in with them earlier when Grandma died. Grandpa wasn't too old, but sometimes he acted like it. I guess it came from that long, drawn-out transition from horse riding and breeding out in the wild country to reservation life in buggies, dirt roads, and cars. He walked slowly everywhere he went; he and Aunt Greta complemented each other that way.

Eventually, Aunt Greta became interested in tribal politics and threatened to run for tribal council, so Grandpa changed her Indian name from Little Girl Heart to Old Woman Walking, which he had called Grandma when she was alive. Aunt Greta didn't mind. In fact, she was proud of her new name. Little Girl Heart was her baby name, she said. When Grandpa died a couple of years later she was all alone. She decided tribal politics wasn't for her but began teaching Indian culture and language classes. That's when I walked into her life like a newborn Mathew or Grandpa or the baby she never had. She had so much love and knowledge to share, which she passed on to me naturally and freely; she received wages for teaching others. But that was gesticulation, she said.

My home life and academic life improved a lot after I had moved in with Aunt Greta. Dad and his wife had a baby boy, and then a girl, but I didn't see too much of them. It was like we were strangers living a quarter mile from one another. Aunt Greta and I went on vacations together from the time I graduated from the eighth grade. We were trailblazers, she said, because our ancestors never traveled very far from the homeland.

The first year we went to Maryhill, Washington, which is about a ten-hour drive from our reservation home in Park City, and saw the imitation Stonehenge Monument. We arrived there late in the evening because we had to stop off in every other town along the road to eat, whether or not we were hungry, because that was Aunt Greta's way and Grandma's and all the other old ladies of the tribe. You have to eat to survive, they would say. It was almost dark when we arrived at the park. We saw the huge outlines of the massive hewn stones placed in a circular position and towering well over our heads. We stood small and in awe of their magnificence, especially seeing darkness fall upon us. Stars grew brighter and we saw them more keenly as time passed. Then they started falling, dropping out of the sky to meet us where we stood. I could see the power of Aunt Greta protruding through her eyes; if I had power I wouldn't have to explore, physically, the sensation I imagined her feeling. She said nothing for a long time. Then, barely audible, she murmured something like, "I have no teepee. I need no cover. This moment has been waiting for me here all this time." She paused. Then, "I wasn't sure what I would find here, but I'm glad we came. I was going to say something goofy like 'we should have brought the teepee and we could call upon Coyote to come and knock over these poles so we could drape our canvas over the skeleton and camp!' But I won't. I'm just glad we came here."

"Oh no, you aren't flipping out on me, are you?" I ribbed her. She always said good Indians remember two things: their humor and their history. These are the elements that dictate our culture and our survival in this crazy world. If these are somehow destroyed or forgotten, we would be doomed to extinction. Our power gone. And she had the biggest, silliest grin on her face. She said, "I want to camp right here!" and I knew she was serious.

We camped in the car, in the parking lot, that night. But neither of us slept until nearly daybreak. She told me Coyote stories and Indian stories and asked me what I planned to do with my life. "I want to be like you," I told her. Then she reminded me that I had a Dad to think about, too, and that maybe I should think about taking up his trade. I thought about a lot of stories I had heard about boys following in their father's footsteps—good or bad—and I told Aunt Greta that I wasn't too sure about living on the reservation and working at the agency all my life. Then I tried to sleep, keeping in mind everything we had talked about. I was young, but my Indian memory was good and strong.

On our way home from Maryhill we stopped off at Coyote's Sweathouse down by Soap Lake. I crawled inside the small cavernous stone structure and Aunt Greta said to make a wish for something good. She tossed a coin inside before we left the site. Then we drove through miles of desert country and basalt cliffs and canyons, but we knew we were getting closer to home when the pine trees starting weeding out the sagebrush, and the mountains overrode the flatland.

Our annual treks after that brought us to the Olympic Peninsula on the coast and the Redwood Forest in northern California; Yellowstone National Park in Wyoming and Glacier Park in Montana; and the Crazy Horse/Mount Rushmore Monuments in South Dakota. We were careful in coordinating our trips with pow-wows too. Then we talked about going all the way to Washington, D.C., and New York City to see the sights and how the other half lived, but we never did.

After high-school graduation we went to Calgary for a pow-wow and I got into trouble for drinking and fighting with some local Indians I had met. They talked me into it. The fight occurred when a girlfriend of one of the guys started acting very friendly toward me. Her boyfriend got jealous and started pushing me around and calling me names; only after I defended myself did the others join in the fight. Three of us were thrown into the tribe's makeshift jail. Aunt Greta was not happy when she came to pay my bail. As a matter of fact, I had never seen her angry before. Our neighbors at the campground thought it was funny that I had been arrested and thrown into jail and treated the incident as an everyday occurrence. I sat in the car imagining my own untimely death. I was so sick.

After dropping the ear poles, I watched Aunt Greta take down the rest of the teepee with the same meticulousness with which we had set it up. She went around the radius of the teepee removing wooden stakes from the ground that held fast the teepee's body to the earth. Then she stood on a folding chair to reach the pins that held the face of the teepee together. She folded the teepee into halves as it hung, still, on the center pole. She folded it again and again until it grew clumsy and uneven, then she motioned for me to come and drop the pole so she could untie the fastener that made the teepee our home. Meanwhile, I had to drop all skeletal poles from the sky and all that remained were a few holes in the ground and flattened patches of grass that said we had been there. I stood looking over the crowd. Lots of people had come from throughout Canada and the northern states for the pow-wow. Hundreds of people sat watching the war dance. Other people watched the stick-games and card games. But what caught my attention were the obvious drunks in the crowd. I was 'one of them' now.

Aunt Greta didn't talk much while we drove home. It was a long, lonely drive. We stopped only twice to eat cold, tasteless meals. Once in Canada and once stateside. When we finally got home, Aunt Greta said, "Good night," and went to bed. It was only eight o'clock in the evening. I felt a heavy calling to go talk to Dad about what had happened. So I did.

He was alone when I arrived at his house. As usual I walked

through the front door without knocking, but immediately heard him call out, "Son?"

"Yeah," I said as I went to sit on a couch facing him. "How did you know it was me?"

He smiled, said hello, and told me a father is always tuned in to his son. Then he sensed my hesitation to speak and asked, "What's wrong?"

"I got drunk in Calgary." My voice cracked. "I got into a fight and thrown in jail too. Aunt Greta had to bail me out. Now she's mad at me. She hasn't said much since we packed to come home."

"Did you tell her you were sorry for screwing up?" Dad asked.

"Yeah, I tried to tell her. But she clammed up on me."

"I wouldn't worry about it," Dad said. "This was bound to happen sooner or later. You really feel guilty when you take that first drink and get caught doing it. Hell, when I got drunk the first time, my Mom and Dad took turns preaching to me about the evils of drinking, fornication, and loose living. It didn't stop me though. I was one of those smart asses who had to have his own way. What you have to do is come up with some sort of reparation. Something that will get you back on Greta's good side."

"I guess that's what got to me. She didn't holler or preach to me. All the while I was driving I could feel her staring at me." My voice strengthened. "But she wouldn't say anything."

"Well, Son. You have to try to imagine what's going through her mind too. As much as I love you, you have been Greta's boy since you were kneehigh to a grasshopper. She has done nothing but try to provide all the love and proper caring that she can for you. Maybe she thinks she has done something wrong in your upbringing. She probably feels more guilty about what happened than you. Maybe she hasn't said anything because she isn't handling this very well either." Dad became a little less serious before adding, "Of course, Greta's been around the block a time or two herself."

Stunned, I asked, "What do you mean?"

"Son, as much as Greta's life has changed, there are some of us who remember her younger days. She liked drinking, partying, and loud music along with war dancing, stick-games, and pow-wows. She got along wherever she went looking for a good time. She was one of the few who could do that. The rest of us either took to drinking all the time, or we hit the pow-wow circuit all straight-faced and sober, never mixing up the two. Another good thing about Greta was that when she found her mate and decided to settle down, she did it right. After she married Mathew she quit running around." Dad smiled, "Of course, Mathew may have had some influence on her behavior, since he worked for the alcohol program."

"I wonder why she never remarried?" I asked.

"Some women just don't," Dad said authoritatively. "But she never had a shortage of men to take care of. She had your Grandpa —and YOU!" We laughed. Then he continued, "Greta could have had her pick of any man on the reservation. A lot of men chased after her before she married, and a lot of them chased after her after Mathew died. But she never had time for them."

"I wonder if she would have gotten married again if I hadn't moved in on her?"

"That's a question only Greta can answer. You know, she may work in tribal programs and college programs, but if she had to give it all up for one reason in the world, it would be you." Dad became intent, "You are her bloodline. You know that? Otherwise I wouldn't have let you stay with her all these years. The way her family believes is that two sisters coming from the same mother and father are the same. Especially blood. After your Mother died and you asked to go and live with your Aunt, that was all right. As a matter of fact, according to her way, we were supposed to have gotten married after our period of mourning was over."

"You—married to Aunt Greta!" I half-bellowed and again we laughed.

"Yeah. We could have made a hell of a family, don't you think?" Dad tried steadying his mood. "But, you know, maybe Greta's afraid of losing you too. Maybe she's afraid that you're entering manhood and that you'll be leaving her. Like when you go away to college. You are still going to college, aren't you?"

"Yeah. But I never thought of it as leaving her. I thought it more like going out and doing what's expected of me. Ain't I supposed to strike out on my own one day?"

"Yeah. Your leaving your family and friends behind may be expected, but like I said, 'you are everything to Greta,' and maybe she has other plans for you." Dad looked down to the floor and I caught a glimpse of graying streaks of hair on top of his head. Then he asked me which college I planned on attending.

"One in Spokane," I answered. "I ain't decided which one yet."

Then we talked about other things and before we knew it his missus and the kids were home. Junior was nine, Anna Lee eight; they had gone to the last day of the tribe's celebration and carnival in Nespelem, which was what Aunt Greta and I had gone to Calgary to get away from for once. I sat quietly and wondered what Aunt Greta must have felt for my wrongdoing. The kids got louder as they told Dad about their carnival rides and games and prizes they had won. They shared their goodies with him and he looked to be having a good time eating popcorn and cotton candy.

I remembered a time when Mom and Dad brought me to the carnival. Grandpa and Grandma were with us. Mom and Dad stuck me on a big, black merry-go-round horse with flaming red nostrils and fiery eyes. Its long, dangling tongue hung out of its mouth. I didn't really want to ride that horse, but I felt I had to because Grandpa kept telling Mom and Dad that I belonged on a real horse and not some wooden thing. I didn't like the horse, when it hit certain angles it jolted and scared me even more. Mom and Dad offered me another ride on it, but I refused.

"Want some cotton candy?" Junior brought me back to reality. "We had fun going on the rides and trying to win some prizes. Here, you can have this one." He handed me one of his prizes. And, "Are you gonna stay with us tonight?"

I didn't realize it was after eleven o'clock.

"You can sleep in my bed," Junior offered.

"Yeah. Maybe I will, Little Brother." Junior smiled. I bade everyone good night and went to his room and pulled back his top blanket revealing his Star Wars sheets. I chuckled at the sight of them before lying down and trying to sleep on them. This would be my first time sleeping away from Aunt Greta in a long time. I still felt tired from my drinking and the long drive home, but I was glad to have talked to Dad. I smiled in thinking that he said he loved me, because Indian men hardly ever verbalize their emotions. I went to sleep thinking how alone Aunt Greta must have felt after I had left home and promised myself to return there as early as I could.

I ate breakfast with the family before leaving. Dad told me one last thing that he and Aunt Greta had talked about sometime before. "You know, she talked about giving you an Indian name. She asked me if you had one and I said 'no.' She talked about it and I thought maybe she would go ahead and do it too, but her way of doing this is: boys are named for their father's side and girls are named for their mother's. Maybe she's still waiting for me to give you a name. I don't know."

"I remember when Grandpa named her, but I never thought of having a name myself. What was the name?" I asked.

"I don't remember. Something about stars."

Aunt Greta was sitting at the kitchen table drinking coffee and listening to an Elvis album when I got home. Elvis always made her lonesome for the old days or it cheered her up when she felt down. I didn't know what to say, but showed her the toy totem pole Junior had given me.

"That's cute," she said. "So you spent the night at the carnival?"

"No. Junior gave it to me." I explained. "I camped at Dad's."

"Are you hungry?" she was about to get up from the table.

"No. I've eaten." I saw a stack of pancakes on the stove. I hesitated another moment before asking, "What's with Elvis?"

"He's dead!" she said and smiled, because that's what I usually said to her. "Oh well, I just needed a little cheering up, I guess."

I remember hearing a story about Aunt Greta that happened a long time ago. She was a teenager when the Elvis craze hit the reservation. Back then hardly any families had television sets, so they couldn't see Elvis. But when his songs hit the airwaves on the radio the girls went crazy. The guys went kind of crazy too—but they were pissed off crazy. A guy can't be that good looking and talented too, they claimed. They were jealous of Elvis. Elvis held a concert in Seattle and my Mom and Aunt Greta and a couple other girls went to it. Legend said that Elvis kissed Aunt Greta on the cheek during his performance and she took to heart the old 'ain't never going to wash that cheek again' promissory and never washed her cheek for a long time and it got chapped and cracked until Grandpa and Grandma finally had to order her to go to the clinic to get some medicine to clean up her face. She hated them for a while, still swearing Elvis would be her number one man forever.

"How's your Dad?"

"He's all right. The kids were at the carnival when I got to his house, so we had a nice, long visit." I paused momentarily before adding, "And he told me some stories about you too."

"Oh?" she acted concerned even though her crow's feet showed.

"Yeah. He said you were quite a fox when you were young. And he said you probably could have had any man you wanted before you married Uncle Mathew, and you could have had any man after Uncle Mathew died. So, how come you never snagged yourself another husband?"

Aunt Greta sat quietly for a moment. I could see her slumping into the old way of doing things which said you thought things through before saying them. "I suppose I could have had my pick of the litter. It's just that after my old man died I didn't want anyone else. He was so good to me that I didn't think I could find any better. Besides, I had you and Grandpa to care for, didn't I? Have I ever complained about that?"

"Yeah," I persisted, "but haven't you ever thought about what might have happened if you had gotten married again? You might have done like Dad and started a whole new family. Babies, even!"

Aunt Greta was truly embarrassed. "Will you get away from here with talk like that. I don't need babies. Probably won't be long now and you'll be bringing them home for me to take care of anyhow."

Now I was embarrassed. We got along great after that initial conversation. It was like we had never gone to Calgary and I had never gotten on to her wrong side at all. We were like kids rediscovering what it was worth to have a real good friend go away for awhile and then come back. To be appreciative of each other, I imagined Aunt Greta might have said.

Our trip to Calgary happened in July. August and September found me dumbfounded as to what to do with myself college-wise. I felt grateful that Indian parents don't throw out their offspring when they reach a certain age. Aunt Greta said it was too late for fall term and that I should rest my brain for awhile and think about going to college after Christmas. So I explored different schools in the area and talked to people who had gone to them. Meanwhile, some of my friends were going to Haskell Indian Junior College in Kansas. Aunt Greta frowned upon my going there. She said it was too far away from home, people die of malaria there, and if you're not drunk, you're just crazy. So I stuck with the Spokane plan.

That fall Aunt Greta was invited to attend a language seminar in Portland. She taught Indian language classes when asked to. So we decided to take a side trip to our old campsite at Stonehenge. This time we arrived early in the morning and it was foggy and drizzling rain. The sight of the stones didn't provide the feeling we had experienced earlier. To us, the sight seemed to be just a bunch of rocks standing, overlooking the Columbia River, a lot of sagebrush, and two state highways. It didn't offer us feelings of mysticism and power anymore. Unhappy with the mood, Aunt Greta said we might as well leave; her words hung heavy on the air.

We stayed in Portland for a week and then made it a special point to leave late in the afternoon so we could stop by Stonehenge again at dusk. So with careful planning we arrived with just enough light to take a couple pictures and then darkness began settling in. We sat in the car eating baloney sandwiches and potato chips and drinking pop because we were tired of restaurant food and we didn't want people staring at us when we ate. That's where we were when an early evening star fell. Aunt Greta's mouth fell open, potato chip crumbs clung to the sides of her mouth. "This is it!" she squealed in English, Indian, and English again. "Get out of the car, Son," and she half pushed me out the door. "Go and stand in the middle of the circle and pray for something good to happen to you." I ran out and stood waiting and wondering what was supposed to happen. I knew better than to doubt Aunt Greta's wishes or superstitions. Then the moment came to pass.

"Did you feel it?" she asked as she led me back to the car.

"I don't know," I told her because I didn't think anything had happened.

"I guess it just takes some people a little longer to realize," she said.

I never quite understood what was supposed to have happened that day. A couple months later I was packing up to move to Spokane. I decided to go into the accounting business, like Dad. Aunt Greta quizzed me hourly before I was to leave whether I was all right and if I would be all right in the city. "Yeah, yeah," I heard myself repeating. So by the time I really was to leave she clued me in on her new philosophy: it wasn't that I was leaving her, it was just that she wouldn't be around to take care of me much anymore. She told me, "Good Indians stick together," and that I should search out our people who were already there, but not forget those who were still at home.

After I arrived in Spokane and settled down I went home all too frequently to actually experience what Aunt Greta and everyone told me. Then my studies got so intense that I didn't think I could travel home as much anymore. So I stayed in Spokane a lot more than before. Finally it got so I didn't worry as much about the folks at home. I would be out walking in the evening and know someone's presence was with me. I never bothered telephoning Dad at his office at the agency; and I never knew where or when Aunt Greta worked. She might have been at the agency or school. Then one day Dad telephoned me at school. After asking how I was doing, he told me why he was calling. "Your Aunt Greta is sick. The doctors don't know what's wrong with her yet. They just told me to advise her family of the possibility that it could be serious." I only half heard what he was saying. "Son, are you there?"

"Yeah."

"Did you hear me? Did you hear what I said?"

"Yeah. I don't think you have to worry about Aunt Greta though. She'll be all right. Like the old timers used to say, 'she might go away for awhile, but she'll be back,' " and I hung up the telephone unalarmed.

KING KUKA

A Blackfeet Indian from Montana, King Kuka enjoys writing mostly as a hobby. King is a full-time professional artist and devotes most of his time and efforts to various art forms.

King's art has won him numerous awards and international acclaim. Although he is perhaps most well known for his impressionistic Native American watercolors, King also works in oils, pastels, and has produced stone and bronze sculptures. In addition to his frequent shows, his permanent public collections include the Thomas Gilcrease Institute of American History and Art, Tulsa, Oklahoma; National Museum of Man, Ottawa, Canada; Heye Foundation, New York; AmerIndian Circle, Washington, D.C.; Heard Museum, Phoenix; Deutsches Museum, Munich, Germany; and Museum of the Plains Indian, Browning, Montana.

An accomplished writer as well, King's poetry has appeared in *The Whispering Wind* (Doubleday), *Voices of the Rainbow* (Viking), *The First Skin Around Me* (Territorial Press), *The Remembered Earth* (Red Earth Press), and *Literature and Life* (Scott, Foresman, & Co.).

FOR THE OLD MEN THEN AND NOW

The old man sits in his rocker now dreaming,
his face carved into a relief
of the bad lands his ancestors roamed.

So let him sleep
let him slumber
let him live again in dreams
of times time can't erase.

Painted ponies, painted lodges
music sung on painted drums.
One, two songs
to warm his heart.

So let him sleep
let him slumber
let him ride on
ponies 'cross the land.

His ancestors traveled across
these grassy plains and sage for
hundreds and hundreds of years following
the great herds and worshipping Natosi.

Now in dreams
it passes slow.
So let him sleep
let him slumber
let him live in dreams
of times time can't erase.

ALL MEDICINE

Still,
Somewhere
There is one who sees beyond.
He sees over,
he sees through.
The one sees beyond even no hope.
This one sees tomorrow.
The black-calf moon to the
ripe berry moon to the trees
popping moon to the green-grass moon
to black-calf moon again.

This one knows your time to the sand hills,
your time to give back to mother earth,
your time for the sun journey.

This one they call holy medicine,
he is all medicine,
still
somewhere
among the hills
among the people.

This one you will know
whose heart still beats.
Drum heart
sees beyond.
He is all holy medicine.

UNTITLED

Like a passing dream
does a memory seem,
meditation about you.

Touch sand in sunlight
or a moon-bright summer night,
feel my song to you.

With the sun in my eyes
or stars in summer skies,
hear my invocation to you.

Hear the cry of floating hawk
the scream of mystic eagle talk
and pity the spirit of this your child.

JUNE MCGLASHAN

In March 1987, I received a letter from Alaska writer, June McGlashan. She wrote, "I was born in Akutan, Alaska. I have lived in the Aleutians all of my life. The natives here are Aleuts. I find the way of life here is unique. We have the most terrible weather in the state—blowing up to 100 mph during the winter at times. The Aleuts live off the sea. They are able to hunt in all types of weather; stories have been passed through villages and through generations of natives.

"Not only is the weather drastic, so is the scenery. Tall mountains encircle much of the villages, making the Aleutians a picturesome place to live.

"My poetry is based on my life here."

June has published her poems in *Calapooya Collage* and in the *Institute of Alaska Native Arts Journal*. She lives in Akutan, Alaska, and is the mother of two small children.

NIGHT AFTER THE STORM

My cheeks burn outside
the first real storm kept.

Late in the break of daylight,
Morning sky blush for
the sun.

Winter ravens become silent,
as the seaotters again claim village
harbors.

The dogs curl into tight balls
of fur. Seagulls stand on
one foot, warm the other.

Every natural Being takes
a bite of winter fever.

EVER HAVE ONE OF THOSE DAYS?

When the world seems perfect and
no one would change it for you.

To touch a chiseled mountain
and feel proud of a carved
wood seal from Snake-the-carver.

The oil stove's out of fuel,
can't cook right.
But the old man comes in
smiling and laughs.

Ever walk to the goose—
smell its burning fuel.
Let steambath smoke
blow in your face.

Dog jumps on me,
gets fur stuck over
all my clothing.
And he talks a happy bark.

Then night approaches,
My man brings in a trout
and hugs me with slimy hands.
Ever have one of those days?

THE WAIT

I watch the South into
the Akun Pass.
Every day, night; even
though I know it is
not time yet.

The winds begin to williwaw.
Colder snow piles on
my doorstep.
The sunrise is red.

I hang my sweater
by an oil stove.
Again it will be
warm.

The fleet arrives,
I feel forever
Each slip across the
bay. All as silent as
the other.

They say I never smile. I never
did.

AFRAID

Afraid as a child,
dark attics—spider country
webs drooping in corners/
ceiling.

Afraid of sleeping in dark,
Drunks sneak upstairs,
& touch secret places.
A dog that bit my leg forever.

Afraid to die
In open sea, where
no man finds me
and rests my bones home.

Afraid to be afraid,
replacing it with
anger, resentment or
a stronger solid self.

DEVIL'S NIGHT

Holiday, evil day.
Men dress as creatures
of imagination.
Their faces held masks,
secretly.

At night women and children
remain indoors.
If anyone dares to
go outside,
Men would frighten them.

Dances, songs of the hideous sound.
Rhyme with the evening wind.
Men return home after winds die.

Women speak of evil happenings.
Depend on men for strength and support.
The men put the spears by the door.

A TRUE STORY

This story I tell is of our sister,
daughter, and dear friend Justina.

They say there were too
many pots on board.
It is why the crabber sank.

A female cook, five men were on board.
In the middle of the Bering/Pacific Ocean.
Captain said, "May day . . . may day!!!"
Panic to have heard,
Blood dropped down to the feet
of all who listen.

Imagine the despair,
A nightmare, scramble in circles.
A screaming voice began to unmask
the danger about.

In a matter of minutes, hours
Disaster sank, as if cursed for this destiny.
Men dove into survival suits.
The cook, a strainful shock.
Terror spoke in her eyes.
Five men! Where are they now?
A suit for the lady,
Someone attempt.

Her small frail body
Shudders in bewilderment.

The boat left its ground.
Buried itself, along with
a Woman . . . Five men safe.

SEAGULL EGG STORY

(Old man Larry Mensoff told this story)

It snowed until the end of May.
It was a bad winter. A long winter.
The snowflakes came down thick and large.
I went out in a skiff with my nephew.
We could not see anything,
but used our compass and
recognized rocks and beaches.

We stayed out all afternoon
Finding the seagulls' "hot spot."

No one thought we would be able
to find any seagull eggs in the snow.

We came back to town.
I showed everyone two buckets
of yellow grass and green
Seagull eggs.

They shook their heads in disbelief.

DIAN MILLION

"I was born in 1950 near Nenana, Alaska, and grew up in Alaska and Oregon. I am Tanana River Athabascan. I have worked at a lot of jobs: maid, cannery worker, nurses' aide, and more recently with Indian programs. I have written all my life, and what I write about are the sincere things that are on all of our minds these days. I want our people to flourish and to be able to live in a good way as they see fit. I do not want to see people destroyed because their subsistence lifestyles are standing in the way of "manifest destiny." There is a dangerous mentality in the reckless way the earth is being treated at this time."

THE HIGHWAY

All the way down I-5 I hear the wheels
underneath
the concrete we follow

they tell me ice had barely retreated
from the northern hemisphere
in the last millennium
when our people came to the river

in the spring we sang to the fish
between the Tanana and the Columbia
each leap of
wild water
a rain of silver so infinite
we believed
it could not end

we followed what the river told us
murmuring in our sleep, answering the
call,
answering each whisper from winged and
finned
and antlered brethren into
all the seasons
all of our spirits mingled
on the banks;
imprinted on the sides of
countless gorges and crevices
where the scaffolding
clings like spider webbing

old names
Minto
Celilo
we are parked along I-5
on the Oregon side across from
Cooks Landing

we can almost hear the dam;
we can hear the diesel trucks
from a long way off but I do not
think you can hear
salmon.

my mother looks up at the river
and I know she is listening;
she hushes my little brother
who is playing with a toy diesel truck.
we get back into the pick-up
and return to the highway.

II. The Call of the Wild: He Went to Town
I woke up
thinking that I was in Sitka:
it was the rain of course, the cold
intruding into minds and lungs
rain
which in Oregon
falls in heavy fine mists: great sweeping hands
of spray
that eventually reach in and
envelop you
while freezing under the bridge, huddled
next
to the peach box kitchen table
        or standing up next to the wall at Gus's or Club 101
waiting for the light to filter through
the fine beautiful cold rain.

he dreamed
and I dreamed of the fish
dancing
silver and light
he said
its the holidays
take one good shot fire in your
mouth

and promise the ground a swallow
and what does wanting get you

what was wanted
of oneself
of wanting so tense that it
became a vision
changing the gray rain into the
keen
indigo sky.

he would remember pine ridge
and I would think of fairbanks
whatever we saw
it was more real than
this.

who says what is real

III. It Gets Done
They are arresting men and women
on the river now
They say it is for selling illegal fish
I don't know what is illegal
since it is what we do to live.

They don't arrest the white men
who come to the river with their greed
and their alcohol, and their expensive
equipment.
It is a sport to catch the salmon
they say.
I know that the salmon don't come up river
anymore.

The men and the women go out to the river at
night.
Their faces are grim.
The men and women tie themselves
to the scaffolding on long
days and it gets done.

We untie the kerchiefs from our heads and wipe
the sweat down,
but sometimes it is mixed with tears.

we make camp
and listen to the river.

I walk to the edge
of every night thinking

what if the river called
and we were not here.

CURRENCY

watching our
blood
its journey into plasma bags
    laying still on tables
    hearing the coughs and restless movements
of people bleeding for
the seven dollars
which sends us out again
able to face looking for something
this
deep
red fluid that propels our hearts

war is money
the blood spilled to the earth
blood appearing suddenly with no warning
from wounds that we inflict on one another

the blood is the currency
by which we trade our destinies
propels
some to be takers on this world
where

racial memories are named for
the taker:
    Sand Creek
    Bosque Redondo
    Auschwitz
    Cape Town

the lives we remember individually
from
the wars fought for money
to run strip mining
take land
erace entire peoples.

No one left untouched
yet some
remain silent not told
that our blood is currency
that
for seven dollars
or for seven billion
it will never buy one thing back.

INVOCATION

old ones say
only the earth endures

in the beginning before the beginning
we became
perhaps from the stone
or sky:
what is not known

we all uttered a word for human
a soft word unfolding from
the palate
of the earth's great mouth

centuries of emerging
learning
what is human
Dine.

the old people hear it in the wind at night
the land still older
tells them
    do not leave; we have known you well
    your shapes and shades mingled
    all the long night of the earth
so that on these four corners
we know the earth meets.

humans walk toward the fifth world
do not fear
pray to be guided well
do not speak harshly

we know it is not
that the earth is raped; it is unthinkable
the human beings; Dine are gathering here.

what we think we create

our thoughts we must know

earth enduring
life enduring
east enduring
west enduring
north enduring
south enduring

Ground Mother we invoke.

BAINBRIDGE: SHE THINKS OF HOME

encircled
by the crystalline water
she thinks of the north

it is in her
blood
she finds mountains
hallucinating
them in the clouds
caught up

bright
rings of water
she will always
seek
the cool distinct creations
in deep pools

in the spring
fireweed & dandelion
bouquets
for the knotholes
she wandered
unencumbered
sleeping lightly
with the firs
singing high songs in the wind

We walk the earth
she says
It is so learned in the blood
to seek
dark quiet glens
each
a treasure of seed cones
and

mysterious ferns
unfolding

She lays her head upon the
moss
minute world
which knows
to grow
north

She is going north
to wear her hair
as a cape
and dance a good
dance for her mother

NANCY NEAL

Nancy Neal, an Oklahoma native, is a thirty-five-year-old mother of three children: Jack, and twin girls Asenah and Star Beth.

Prior to her surprise blessings she was the Director and Cultural Specialist of the Urban Indian walk-in/out patient Health Clinic for the off-reservation population. She has also served as Universal Member at Large and on the Executive Committee for the American Indian Health Care Association and vice-chaired the Montana Urban Indian Health Care Association.

She has lived in Montana for the past twenty-five years and makes her home in Missoula. Her poetry has appeared in *Calapooya Collage*.

JULIE-ANNA

Tonight I toss and turn three hours.
Jack wants milk
And I feel my cervix low
The moon over the mountain.

A warm breeze from the East
tells me it's your time.

Your baby low in the womb
Ready to enter this world
From before
Where waters rushed last night.

The mill saws late
And trees sing the rip of steel
June bugs gather late August heat
And huddle the back door stoop.

This world stops only for you tonight.
In the morning your babe will wake
Her first morning,
Sing cry her first morning.
And your body.
Sing cry the first morning.

Your body will take you through
Trust the journey of your child
They know where they are going
As the tree grows towards the sun.

Sing cry the first morning.
Sing cry.

CHRISTMAS POEM

It is Christmas Eve
Your ex-wife and children
are fighting.
You snap at me for the last time.
I'm going out I say.

It is rainy, no snow this Christmas
And your children argue over which
Soap opera has the hour glass.
I huddle in this old tipi
Still expect some warmth
From last night's fire.
Slowly gather kindlin
feed that empty pit
One stick at a time.

DUANE NIATUM

Duane Niatum is the author of four volumes of poetry. *Songs for the Harvester of Dreams*, published in 1981 by the University of Washington Press, won the American Book Award in 1982 from The Before Columbus Foundation. In the Spring of 1990, Holy Cow Press published his new collection, *Drawings of the Song Animals: New and Selected Poems*. He also publishes short fiction and essays which have appeared in magazines and anthologies. He was born in Seattle, Washington, and has spent most of his life there. In June 1983, he was invited to participate in Rotterdam's International Poetry Festival. His poems, stories, and essays have been translated into more than ten languages including Italian, Dutch, and Russian. In 1975 he edited an anthology entitled *Carriers of the Dream Wheel* (Harper & Row). It has become the most widely read and known book on contemporary Native American poetry. He has just completed a new anthology entitled *Harper's Anthology of Twentieth Century Native American Poetry* (Harper & Row, 1988). His last teaching job was in the winter of 1985 at the University of Washington. He is of mixed blood and a member of the Klallam Nation of Washington. The Klallam are a Salishan tribe of salmon fishermen. The name means "strong people."

ROUND DANCE*

Sweet Woman, come dance with me,
let's touch earth's center, so no one's a stranger,
I welcome you on this Klallam path
as the flicker does whose tapping beak
is as moon-inlaid as the cedar bark.
O step with me round the fire,
enter the circle the blood sparks,
            the heart unearths.

Please sway and linger like the soil's thistles,
the yellow leaf's season, the flattened shadows.
Oh yes, our drums were carved by the sea,
its mother foam and Thunderbird.
like the blue wind among blue willow,
the surf unites harvest dreams to stars,
deep currents, snipe and coot, starfish and black bass,
                footprints ingrained.

Fox woman, come dance with me,
let's find earth's beach, unravel yourself and tide,
let grass burn ocher, your hands be blue camas,
we'll turn as mischievous as Raven stealing light.
O I am best welcoming a friend.
So let's mingle with guest and ancestor,
Duckabush river and tamahnous, release the abalone
            yearnings, the eyeless flights.

*The round dance is a traditional dance among tribal people throughout America. It is a friendship dance and is meant to break the ice.

SON, THIS IS WHAT I CAN TELL YOU

Time, the mapmaker and the one who peppers
the road with holes deeper than a thunder's crack,
the clown who laughs or cries in the tunnel

by which we stumble until it offers oblivion,
grows louder than the madness drums
as we grow smaller and deafer.
Oh yes, in my vanity and pride I was nourished
like a water ouzel on the iced, tart-red punch
of The-One-Who-Knows—but never tells.

This then is the hurdle that will test
your bones as well as spirit the most:
nothing during these forty-eight years hinted
how the minutes, days, decades can be stopped
from slipping through our fingers like jelly
as we drift in absence. For what lights
the future to the past is blacker
than Killer Whale's fin and as indifferent
to our story as our birth.

Recently I picked myself up from a fall
as slow as a face focusing on a yellow photograph,
yet lighter than a dragonfly's wing.
It was a night I heard for the first time
the bird that chanted from my ribcage
an answer to death: *not yet, not yet*.
Son, its voice hummed a reality more present
than all the people and art discovered in the sky,
country, sea, river, city, and heart.

These fingers change the puzzle, our lives,
shape, color, direction, and name what
we see before they can live with our ashes
or their own. So time shows the way
to drop into ourselves like the turtle
on its back, to want merely the half-notes
of Venus and the stars, to be the remains
of night, its dancer dangling
from the sky's daisy-chain web.

And like your mother's, there's a woman's embrace,
there are the arts, the shield of love.

I loved your mother because she gave me a gift—
you, and the will to be soft and not cruel,
a man and not a machine, a failure
but a carrier of the moon's. Your gentle
mother set loose a song sparrow that flew
through my sleep's evergreens.
From such a field I can believe the diamond-cutting
fiction of a rising sun.

So my son who takes a different road
away from the red cedar and yellow pine,
the road that brings me to my gnarled elders,
the earth and shore of my Klallam family—
try remembering when your anger is lifted
like fog from a coastal storm,
I cannot call you back, cannot offer what
wasn't theirs, the popping fire
and butterfly dancers of this place.

So when you roll like riverbed gravel,
fall like the sun through trailing current,
see more as the feather than antler,
you will find that only the bald eagle
and salmon, forest and sea can call you back,
only nature carves the totem of the spine's
four-knots. Then the wounds I gave you
as a child will drop like mountain rain
into my hands. For your father was seasoned
on salt air and the longhouse stories
clotted in blood rage.

YELLOW PINE CLIFF SONG

What keeps my cousins and myself
returning to this Hadlock path,
what draws us home before dark,

when death takes our parents from our arms
is surely to hear on the wind
our great grandmother Oatsa's* stories
of Thunderbird and Crow,
A Young Woman Marries a Sea Being,
or to stand on the bank at Chemakum Creek
when it lures the tyee salmon
with the counter-motions of ancestors
in the gravel-garden of their beginnings.

O we will dance down the hill
to the beach and wait for the wind
in the yellow pines to shake with her song
she sang as we all picked chokecherries
into dusk, on the day she teased
her husband, Niatum, who had stood
on the cliff's edge swinging his cane
at us who had stolen his canoe
to paddle beyond the willow swish
of his anger, the cackle of crows
and herring gulls gliding on an air
stream above Skunk Island.

*Oatsa is the author's maternal great grandmother's "Indian" name and Niatum is his maternal great grandfather's Indian name.

OLD TILLICUM

(for Francis Patsy, my grandfather)

A timber blue haze dissolves
on chokecherry leaves, thimbleberry, and the ants'
footprints at the beginning of the thicket.
Pebbles in the water leap before the salmon
in the current; the brush keeps us guessing
at the steps of the elk kicking dirt
on its run down the canyon.

The sky lifts my alder-smoked frame
like an unbroken impulse of the mountain,
Memp-ch-ton,* to pause with goldenrod, willow
and blue jay flying across the river of my people.

An old Klallam, I sit with my grandson
while from the fern distances the Elwha rushes
seaward. I watch for the voices
of the river to show him the currents to manhood,
strengthen his green awkwardness,
flush his cheek with spruce light,
and promise my brittle bones a few more moons.

First mountain to choose his ancestors,
mirrored in the rapids and the falling sun,
it dwarfs the white firs that once spread
the village fires like a family of sap and lichen.
Pitch-dry with age I am here
to see that my daughter's son starts
the long journey back to the clearing of Old Patsy,
sings for me the story of when Old Patsy
pulled in a net swimming with herring,
the net that will pull him on like the tide.
As a boy once frightened of the surf's
crack below the hemlock, pine, and cedar,
our evening walks by lantern to the circle
and home of Young and Lucy Patsy,
he now disappears beyond the edge
of the mountain's sunset; a fox running shadows.

By the time the quail roost and the dusk
is mute on the ridge above the ravine,
I tell him of the legend of the seven brothers
that named the village long burned to ash,
how these ancestors danced into the fire

*Memp-ch-ton is the name the Klallam call their sacred mountain. The Eur/
American name is Mt. Olympus.

to forget. And like their totem to the Thunderbird,
the moon drifts full height into the next horizon,
returning to its birth.

Perhaps asking us all to touch the earth
from this dawn to the next on through summer,
it looks as if his guardian spirit
is answering his chant to let him carry home
for good what the water drum has offered.

As his grandfather I rise too late
to return home with little crow. Instead, I hear
his first jump through chance's hoop.

NILA NORTHSUN

"i am a shoshone-chippewa living on my reservation in fallon, nevada. a single parent with three kids, i commute 150 miles a day to work in a reno warehouse 6 days a week 10 hours a day with *no* time to even think of writing.

i used to write a lot, what seems to have been many lifetimes ago. a couple of books, many anthologies here and in europe, a hundred small press publications. and though i am not actively writing now, i'm busy living it all & keeping my eyes & ears open.

it'll get to paper eventually.

p.s. In '89, I became the Social Services Director for my tribe. Wow, you should hear these stories."

WHAT THE ANTHROS DON'T HEAR

about the sundance
this one anyway
is the laughter
i'm a woman in camp
i help the men
gather sage for their
head, wrists, & ankles
i go to the yardage store
for their colors
i buy clothesline, or hemp
that they use when they
tie to the center pole & pierce
onetime i almost bought macrame yarn
cause they were out of everything else
or if they forget matches
or a pocketknife or buckskin
i get it for them
then i enjoy their company
eavesdrop on their jokes
one guy is making piercing skewers
for somebody else
it is all crooked & splintery
they laugh & say he won't feel it
cause when they lay him on the
buffalo robe
he'll faint anyway
another wants me to cook his in oil
cause the last time a splinter
got infected
so we laugh about me stir-frying
his piercing sticks
does he want it rare or well-done?
they joke about tying somebody
with elastic so when he tries
to break from the pole

he'll bounce all over the lodge
they joke about the size of the skewers
how some are so skinny like beading needles
& some are macho with skewers as big as
their thumb
they laugh about everything
i keep bringing coffee & pop
for soon it will get more serious
they will build the sundance lodge
begin their fast
then dance & pray for four days
but even then
during short breaks
i can hear them laughing
& everybody feels so good.

SOMETIMES

life isn't so hard
occasionally
to stop
a moment
& not interact
helps clear the air
to think of nobody but
myself
is nice
to catch some small warmth
from a winter sun

i feel kind of pretty today
my body feels strong
i danced & watched
my silhouette on the walls
i wished i had a big mirror

now i'm sitting outside
in a chair on the porch
it's cold but i'm bundled
i feel good
not moving
once in awhile
looking around
not bored or lonely
but peaceful & contented

unlike yesterday
i was bitchy & grouchy
sometimes i like to
hear myself holler
nobody else does
but that was yesterday

life was harder.

HUNTER

he shoots things
he's a hunter
he's proud of it
he says he eats
whatever he shoots
& he does
unfortunately
he'll eat anything.

HANBLECHIA

we talked quietly about it
he's done it a few times
part of an involved sioux
belief system
the vision quest
a time for getting in
touch with yourself
and your creator
and maybe spirit helpers
but i suppose unless
you've actually gone through it
it's hard to really explain
just like childbirth
each time unique
& to each person different
he said that it's like that
you don't go thru the pain
of childbirth just for its
own sake
but as a way to the end goal
as the new baby enriches &
changes lives
so can the revelations &
experience of hanblechia
which made a lot of sense
i had always said i would
or could never handle what
i thought was pure torture
no food or water
no fire
just a blanket maybe
& you & the great outdoors
sitting in one spot
for four days & nights
talking to yourself &

the great spirit
i felt too weak and scared
i thought i might die
freeze to death
get drug off by wild animals
wither & cave in
or hallucinate so badly
werewolves would get me
scare myself to death
& i still kind of think that
but then
i survived childbirth
3 times
the results were worth it
a spiritual birth
might be worth a try.
it's always the unknown
that's the scariest.

TWO WORLDS

given time
we may become more alike
but for now
i'm dressed in
two pairs of socks &
layers of other clothes
sitting on the back porch
with no moon, a porchlight,
a rum & coke, a pen & paper
listening to country music
while he

sits naked in a sweatlodge
praying to grandfather
jumping in the river afterwards
then he'll jog home 4 miles
& make love to me
& our worlds come together.

SANDRA OSAWA

Sandra Osawa is from the Makah Tribe in the northwest corner of Washington State. She began writing poetry in the fourth grade and continued writing while working with Professors Vern Rutsala and William Stafford at Lewis and Clark College where she graduated in English. Sandra worked extensively for the Makah Tribe in the 1960s and spearheaded a drive to retain Makah culture through the revival of songs, dances, and language classes. Poems such as "The Makahs" grew out of this time period. She later produced and directed a ten-part television series for KNBC-TV on the Native American and won an "Outstanding Producer's Award" from the station. She is currently an independent producer/writer and owns a graphics and video company, Upstream Productions, with her husband, Yasu Osawa. They live in Seattle with their two children. She adds that, "I am presently trying to alter my life so I can regain my link with poetry, for to ignore it, is to ignore myself."

THE MAKAHS

We sprang
from salt water
a meeting of waves
Our men hollowed
canoes
from logs
with the bone of whale
and together we rose
as one
but were many
giving thanks to the sea
we were born
startling the birds
into flight while the seagulls
cried
circling the air
and following the strain
of our paddles
moving us
toward land.

Now our men
keep returning to the sea
filled with the rhythm
of salmon
flashing a strange beauty
through dark waters
as silver fins
leap wildly over death
seeking the savage moment
that saves
the young.

Our people will not die.

MY SONG

When my song
is your song
is our song
is one song
There's no song
There's no song
There's no song at all.
When myself
is yourself
is ourself
is one self
There's no self
There's no self
There's no self at all.
Yes, when one becomes two
and two become one
then two minus one
becomes none
becomes
none.

THE CATCH

Indian fishermen
sit
at the mouth
of the Hoko
waiting for the tides
to change.
I watch their nets
forming white patterns
in the darkness
and the night seems
suddenly full

of a strange kind of love
as the river begins
to widen
and the men head
knowingly
toward boats.

TO IGOGARUK

Your body
is rubbed with the smell of fires
smoky
from the sticks of old women
prodding the coals.
The North Wind blows through your mouth
bringing sounds
of a distant village
and men at dawn climbing into boats
as familiar
to them
as their wives.
Now
your black hair looms above me
falling thickly to one side
rich
like the taste of seal oil
and I watch your eyes
seeming to open
on the sight of dog teams
far off
bringing home the news.
There is the clinking of the ice
when it first begins to move
and I see you rising
smooth
like a straight harpoon

sensing a course
as old as the lines
in the hands
of our people.

TWO BROTHERS

The Suez* warriors are gone.
Our great whales have sunk
to the bottom
of the sea
who knows if they will ever come up
again.
The Suez warriors are gone
with the sun's sparkle
and the moon's breath
they are gone
taking the waves' laughter
high upon the beach
and the ocean's roaring
far into itself
they are gone
singing their songs together
into the Indian night
and praying that we might find
our Indian day.

*Suez is a traditional village of the Makahs.

AGNES PRATT

Agnes Pratt was born on December 23, 1945, on the Port Madison Indian Reservation. She writes, "I am Suquamish, descendent of one of Chief Seattle's sub chiefs, who was known as Salmon Bay Curley.

"I have lived on the reservation most of my life. I studied creative writing and painting at the Institute of American Indian Arts and recently graduated from the Northwest College of Art.

"I live in two worlds—a concrete sidewalk leads to my front door, and in my backyard I have a sweat lodge. I view my work as an expression of gratitude towards my creator for allowing me to live one day at a time."

EMPATHY

Our glances spin silver threads
Weaving a web of closeness;
Catching, holding
A love too tenuous for words.
Woven and remembered
In silence, those hours
When time had something
To do with the moon.

Stay, or flee
As you must—
Uncountable the ways
We seek ourselves
I will keep
The interwoven strands of you
As I keep the enduring moon
And its web of shadow.

SO QUICKLY CAME THE SUMMER

Night laid itself down beside the horizon,
The mountain wrapped itself in clouds,
Forest sighed through yellowing leaves
hushed in mourning for dying spring.
So quickly came the summer
When spring departed, she left
A young boy strumming a guitar,
The moon sighing along its strings,
As he slowly walked down the hill.

DEATH TAKES ONLY A MINUTE

Agonies of change
can be heard
in the lonely silence
of a single raindrop
bending a leaf downward.

All this is distant
and will fade further back
when my relatives assemble to haggle
over the price of dying.

SUMMER '76

I caught and held
a song in flight
Saw blue ribbons
of moontide sorrow
I walked toward death
Singing all the time.

MAY 1977

What wondrous vigils
I have kept
in dreamless sleep
Wind storms glide
through darkened skies
thoughts that soar
beyond hours and time
Until at morning
I hold one glittering star
in my hands of sleep.

REVERIE

Along the shore of quiet
Sea waves glide
beneath an ancient moon
Spirit song rhythms . . .
Oh, what longing
to follow
to join that music!

RALPH SALISBURY

"My tribal affiliation is Cherokee, English, and Irish. I mean this as an affirmation, not simply an angry rejoinder to the implicit Euro-American assumption that "tribe" means inferior and, even, sub-human status. To the "civilized" Romans, the "Germanic Tribes" were redindians, fair game for slaughter and plunder. My Cherokee people were tribal and, also, part of the Iroquois and part of humanity. My father was named for an English king, Charles, his mother for Christendom's most famous mother, Mary; her mother bore a Cherokee name, Chicabob. I write often about Cherokee realities, my own, mostly, and those of my family, but our realities are part of humanity's experience—war, race-strife, suffering, human dignity, human idiocy, hate, love. I write out of love for my people and for all people. The contemporary Amer-Anglo development of a Germanic language is a battleground, the only one in which I have won victories significant enough to encourage further battle. It is also a planting-ground. By fighting when I have to and by planting when I can, I try to stay alive, not just as an Indian, not just as an Anglo, but as a human, as myself, and by fighting and planting I hope to help keep others alive."

To Take Life, To Kill

"Everthing matters—everthing!" Seek's uncle began, come back from work, for what would be their fourth and last night. "If one bird finds one flower too few, whole centuries of flocks won't never get born. Because Hummingbird was little, the Spirits didn't notice him bearing their Medicine tobacco off to earth. You ain't full-sized yet, but you are important to what's left of our people, that used to be so many not so long ago. Live good each moment. The inch or so my old leg flinched back from a rattlesnake's strike, has give me the years to be here, telling what's left to tell. It all connects, Seek—Churakee Spirit Bears—apes turning into men, them big, meat-gobbling lizards into little, flower-sucking birds, like them scientists tells us in daughter's books—" Seek thought of shadows moving under nightgown when his cousin primped against dawn window. "It all connects."

This last night was as clear as the first three, the moon low behind pines, the "Firebirds of the Sky" migrating in their formations, as the seasons pursued, while a hungry, sleepy boy—about to die, to become a man—heard—and would live on, hearing and remembering—an old man telling story after story of animal after animal hunted and become the flesh of boys, who would father more children—voice fading, lower and lower, across the lower and lower fire.

Seek awoke, startled.

His uncle was snoring, but there were no other sounds, no cries of nightbirds, no stirring of wind, and, slowly, recognizing the time from the angle of The Big Dipper, Seek realized that what had awakened him was the huge animal's not coming to circle as it had for three nights.

A meteor hurtling, past the pole-star, he remembered his Granny's saying "Fire Panther," but this meteor hurtled on, white light of a bomber—headed to test Russia's radar—or really going to bomb—disappearing into moonlit cloud, leaving a glowing vapor-trail straight as a gold spear thrust into golden whale, the sound of motors rumbling, like distant rolling-thunder, obliterated by explosion.

Sabotage—terrorists—Seek thought, then, as the motor rumbling resumed and the plane lights reappeared, thought sonic-boom, thought gas-leak exploding.

"Just them drunk lumberjacks," Seek's uncle murmured sleepily, breath puffs rising from darkness to glow in moonlight and vanish. "Poaching a deer or shooting each other. Go back to sleep."

Seek almost answered that he couldn't but remembered in time, in time, that he was still supposed to keep silent this one last night.

Owls had surrounded the clearing, and through the light of the moon, that was a round clearing, itself, in clouds, owl after owl dived, to rise with something small writhing in talons, then flew back into the black woods, the huge birds themselves dark as ravens against night sky, and Seek remembered Granny's story of Raven Mockers, witches plunging, crying like ravens and trailing meteor-fire off black wings as they plunged to eat people's hearts and steal the years of others' lives for their own ugly lives.

He lay awake listening to bat wings' knife-slice sounds above him, and then that ceased, the bats bellies full—or maybe the insects had moved down mountain to escape chill.

Across the circle of dark sky encircled by dark trees, the constellation-animals fled whatever was after them or pursued whatever they were pursuing, and Seek could sort of tell by now that it was more or less after midnight because of how far the constellations had moved. He thought of his uncle and other soldiers looking at the stars to see how much more night would have to be endured, and he reminded himself, as his uncle had told him he must, that in this very circle centuries of Cherokee boys had watched the stars moving the last night of their hunger and silence and fear.

Sun a new ball of life, clouds afterbirth puddled on dark mountain-horizon, red hunting-cap held at heart, Seek's uncle threw dawn-crimsoned brown face up to a sky half blaze, half fading night, hair flung back—white cataract—falling to sweat-glazed deerskin jacket-collar, eyes, strained wide, black gleams, lids, tensed, strangely pale amid dark wrinkles, frost stubble of four days without shaving quivering flames in red sunrise, lips rapidly moving, shadowing, uncovering, teeth and glistening tongue, phlegmy, old, first-of-the-day voice intoning "Ha Yi Yu, Great Spirit," the same words which had risen, from frontyard, each morning, into glowing window, awakening Seek, then, "See, now, child dead, man born," voice gradually strengthening to family-time *Bible*-reading voice, chanting, "Waya, Kawa, Seesquaw, Wadi," four times, toward East, North, West, South. "Seekwaya. Well may he live."

Seek, hearing his own full name, in his uncle's strange pronunciation, the first word he'd understood, felt proud.

"Well may he"—hair avalance-snow, flung forward, white-frost stubbled chin seeking dew-glittering brown grass—"die, as a man dies, when he must. Twelve years, already, returning to Earth. Bird Hunter. Pheasant Hunter. Squirrel Hunter soon. Warrior, if need be, in time to come. Keeper of the old paths. Seeker after new. Seekwaya. Nephew to me. And son—son of my brother—son of our people. Seekwaya. Named for our maker of writing, which saved our Cherokee ways from forgetting. Seekwaya. He will be wise and he will be brave and he will be strong. He will live in The People. He will live in The Everlasting Earth. A linden seed falling. A part of the forest. He will live beyond death. It is so."

As they stood side by side, silent, faces raised to sky, out of its own roar, that had been growing in the sunrise, rose the first of this day's bombers—silver monsters to Seek when his bus passed the base hours of highway west of here—this one a distant, tiny gleam, in the head of an enormous serpent fiery in sun—bomber contrail vivid against clouds, like the pawprint-trail which had darkened dewy brown grass.

"That pilot feller done had him his breakfast and gone to work, threatening with his bomb that could cook more people than all the Snake Monster Uktenas and Raven Mocker Witches, which they used to was around here, ever gobbled off'n this earth," Seek's uncle said. "We only going to eat us one squirrel." During the four days and nights his voice had kept going back and forth from preacher talk to plain talk; now, his voice was old and quavery.

Seek, released by his uncle's words, cleared his throat and, afraid it might be unreligious to spit, swallowed, then, his voice sounding strange after long silence, mumbled, "I was scared we was going to get eaten."

Seek's uncle laughed, teeth and whisker stubble white glitters. "That lonesome old bear's been pinning his hopes on my lunch sack ever sincet he was a cub. No berries this late, and, cause he can't fly south like them hummingbirds what been trying to drink from your ears, last night he risked going after those loggers' corn-whisky-mash. The guard was probably so drunk he thought he was shooting a revenue officer in a fur coat, but he managed to wound one paw, as you can see."

In the circle of pressed down grass silvery with dew, each fourth print glistened red.

"Ever awe-tomb when I was a boy, bears some mine-company-feller'd only crippled would devour calves," the old man sighed. "I better lug my big rifle back up here, before this poor, wounded old codger gets so starved he comes down after something slow enough to catch—somebody's lamb, or—school soon to start—somebody's little child."

Dark shape circling in darkness, blood glittering in claw prints—the black dog's teeth tore Seek's arm from his throat.

Startled from dream, Seek looked toward quail-whistle signal, a huge silhouette humped above brambles, becoming a charred stump shadowed black—then looked up in time to glimpse a furry tail, an energetic red flame, among leaves glowing like coals.

Though excited and still confused by his dream of the black dog and the huge black bear and his uncle's big rifle and tomorrow's hunt—he aimed, careful to swivel only head and gun, so as not to alert the squirrel; and, when it moved into sunlight, upside down, tiny black claws dug into gray bark, little black eyes glittering, searching, he squeezed the thin, unfamiliar trigger, gun jolt against shoulder scarcely noticeable, the explosion weak, compared to that of his dad's shotgun; but, like the brilliantly plumaged pheasants, last autumn, awe-tomb, the squirrel crumpled, plunging through glowing leaves, to imprint brown-leaf-covered forest floor, a redgold question-mark, from thick, curved tail to dark dot nose.

"To kill, to take life, they's a difference, they's a world, a whole, big world of difference," Seek heard—his Medicine Vision, Thunder-bolt-Molten-Glow-Volcano-Flow-Cresting-To-Snow-Peak-torrent-ripple engendered, an aeon's instant later, as—impotent rifle deflecting thorns from eyes—he ran, flesh torn by brambles and, in terrified imagination, by teeth, fleeing, body, mind, spirit strained to the utmost, to escape, as long as possible, death.

The old man's shadow gigantic, above his own, Seek knelt and slit, as instructed, up belly, to throat, flayed doll-size legs, then peeled skin and laid it—like a wet, red mitten, tail an orange tassel—on new-fallen, scarlet leaves, the squirrel pelt to be cleaned, salted, stretched and dried, "till late awe-tomb, when cold sets in for good," then tanned in "oak-gall-mash," and stitched into a sheath and mailed—like last month's bus-ticket—"so's you can carry your great uncle's knife, that's now yours."

Mumbling the "thank you," his mother always prompted with "What do you say?" at Christmas, Seek—hoping next to hear, "Your grandpa's rifle, that's now yours"—kept his eyes down and went on cutting white-streaked, pink belly, crimson hands smoking like the innards in morning cold.

"In The Old Time, it used to they was some words, and at my daughter's first passing of blood, Ma knew them to say, and Ma's brother knew, when I first took meat, but the words done gone from my mind like he done gone from earth, and all the honoring and the acknowledging we can do is eat what you taken, put it right back to use in the world, right where you taken it, its own Spirit Place."

Although Seek's uncle had spoken quietly, bluejays' squawking abruptly grew frantic, then went still.

"Pick up your gun!"

Wondering how much was meant by the "your" he'd first hoped to hear four days ago, Seek started wiping his fingers with leaves, thinking he'd get to test his aim on another squirrel just as he'd finished butchering this one, but, startled by hissed "Quick," he bent and, right hand still sticky with blood, grabbed wood gun-stock back of trigger-guard and straightened, just as a huge, dark shape emerged from crimson bushes only fifty paces upslope, its immense body wobbling slightly each time right front paw hit earth, black lips wincing from yellow teeth.

Seek felt his uncle's hand clasp his shoulder, to guide him, backward, between briar tangles, slowly drawing him away, still faced toward the bear, which now put wounded paw onto the squirrel's rear end, pinning it to earth, bit the carcass in half, swallowed and bowed for the other half, the squirrel's tiny, black eyes glittering between huge, yellow teeth a moment, before being gulped down.

The bear's own eyes winced shut, swinging into sun, but twitching black nose guided jaws to glistening innards they'd thrown aside in tearing the body apart.

"Stay real still, awhile, and don't look, or it'll attack," Seek's uncle whispered, as, steaming blue squirrel guts jerking down into throat, the bear raised its blood-smeared muzzle; but Seek had already looked, looked deep, fascinated, hypnotized, into the sunlight-shrunken blacks of the glowing brown eyes; and, with an immense growl, lurching from side to side on all fours, the bear plunged downhill after them.

"Run for dear life," Seek's uncle shouted, huge hand spinning Seek around, jerking him into motion, before letting go.

Seek heard the huge body hurtling after them, tearing through raspberry tangles he and his uncle had to edge between.

"Keep on running, boy, run to beat hell."

Seek ran on, then, as gunshots sounded, turned.

His uncle, automatic rifle straight out at arm's length, was triggering bullets into already bloody eyes, after each shot, withdrawing gun muzzle and stepping back from swipes of pale claws as long as fingers, thrust from black hair, the beast stiffening, rearing taller, at each shot, like a giant blindfolded, with red handkerchief, before firing-squad.

When Seek cried, "You run now, too," the bear went down on all fours and charged his voice.

Brambles, entangling boot laces, toppled Seek's uncle as he spun aside.

The bear stopped, puzzled, paw swiping air, searching for the creature who had destroyed its eyes, bloody head angling brown-burr-encumbered ears, but the old man now lay silent, body curled like a baby's, belly pressed to tangled legs.

Afraid of causing an attack if he moved to try to help, Seek hesitated, till, flared nostrils finding prey, the bear again lurched forward.

Seek lunged and thrust gun-muzzle between black lips gaping just above his uncle's knees; then, as teeth clamped down hard, and jerked him toward swiping paws, he gave one last, desperate shove, felt steel jolt against spine at the back of the throat and fired, seeing, as the rifle was wrenched from his grip, one broken tooth, a jagged iceberg, floating in a torrent of red, claws flashing sunlight above him, as he fell toward scarlet-streaked, black fur, his shadow sending fleas springing away the instant before his nose flattened between ribs, the two bones widening and closing like the blades of a scissors, as the huge body crumpled, knocking both Seek and his half risen uncle backward, threshing bulk pinning them both.

Seek twisted sideways, head and shoulders squeezing between paw and slimy armpit, then clutched vines and dragged himself free of the heavy, desperately contorting belly, just as the bear, weakening, subsided, its last spasm dragging wounded paw over the hand with which Seek's uncle had propped himself, trying to rise.

Four slashes flaring crimson across brown knuckles, the old man laughed—a scared laugh Seek, wounded, would hear from his own lips in seven years—muttered, "My old friend here done put his mark on me, to remember when next we meet, sure did—owed me a little something, too, I reckon," then shook his head, white hair clouding wet black eyes, and, in his awed *Bible*-reading voice, preacher's, more than preacher's—whispered, "I don't have the right words for this neither, but thanks, thanks and God Bless you, you saved me—saved me what's left of my life."

VICKIE SEARS

Vickie L. Sears is a writer, feminist therapist, and teacher living in Seattle, Washington. Her works have appeared in *A Gathering of Spirit: Writing and Art by North American Indian Women*, *Calyx*, *Backbone*, *Gathering Ground: New Writing by Northwest Women of Color*, *The Things that Divide Us: Stories by Women*, *Hear the Silence*, and *Sinister Wisdom*. A volume of her short stories, *Simple Songs*, has been published by Firebrand Books.

She has recently contributed a chapter on sexual abuse to a women's study textbook, *Changing Our Power* (Kendell-Hunt, 1987); two chapters to a book about Lesbian relationships, *Lesbian Couples* (Seal Press, 1988); and two articles on ethics for a text to be published by members of the Feminist Therapy Institute. She is currently working on a novel.

THE ORPHANAGE LOST

It was my secret.
in nights middle
i would wait for cadenced breathing
before reaching for the
sneakers.
laces tied together
they dangled from my neck
as I slid across the cold squared
glass smooth floor
down the hall
into the alcove where waited the
thin French door opening to the fire escape.
sshh
creak it went
rested
slightly
against paper placed on the locking hole
so i could get back in.
i'd step onto the dewfrosted metal
socksoaked wetness curled
around the foot
up the sides
to darken my toes.
it was good.
easing down to the earth
putting on the slender sneakers
i skulked away from the last escape rung
to creep clear of the boys dorm and garage.
once passed
my mind would uncoil
heart pounded in the temples
i could feel the bloodbeating force of
myself and
i ran
ran

sailed cold night air
without sound
wind and i were one
i was a gazelle
an eagle
a grace
leg stretch on stretch
nothing hurt
everything worked together with ease and peace
down
up
down
i could run forever.
65th street was no longer
concrete
forbidden exploration
it was air
wind
mine.
it led to the lake of distant lights and
quiet sounds
to thick grass places where water creatures hid
nourished by water lappings.
i could curl and
know myself as a piece of earth
lay cold and warm at once
feel rhythms that i knew as part of me.
i was lovely there
was the quiet i knew i was
but couldn't be
was the special me no one saw
because i'd be crushed if they did
and could sing it
clear
know the wholeness of myself
while waiting for sky to crack
the world to change

before having to leave
and i ran
ran a singing
ran the sunbrightness of me
back through the frenchdoors
just in time to be
the me others said i should
and was
but my socks stayed wet.

Music Lady

On days of rain, when poetry often came to paper, I'd sneak away from the orphanage, running to leg tautness and chest burn all the way to 15th and 65th streets to the record store. That's where the music lady lived. Where there were sounds that made my poetry seem brighter. Where the music lady smiled under high cheekbones, patted my head, and whispered words of encouragement.

It wasn't an ordinary record store, then or now. It had listening booths and rows of deep wooden forest-green troughs filled with the faces of musicians and instruments. These were the instruments of the big band music my mother liked. Different from the flutes, bells, and drums of my father's family. Different, too, from the silence of the orphanage, except for the dinner bell. Here trumpets and cellos blared in silence from cardboard covers. Grownups strolled the aisles and flicked through the records, like playing cards, choosing their hand of music before taking it to one of the narrow rectangles, each equipped with turntable and speakers, to listen. The soundproofed booths created individual worlds of monophonic magic seeping through the glass doors.

It never really mattered much what was playing, although I began to gravitate to jazz and playful Bach. Bach sounded of creek-skipping water and duck laughs. It was hard for me to understand how a man who dressed with lace edging his jacket and pants, and wearing such a ponderous wig, could have so much fun. Still, I'd walk beside the booths, spiral binder and pencil in hand, searching for just the right music to write near. As casually as a walnut-colored nine-year-old among the tall, mostly white adults could, I'd position myself against a booth's doorjamb and lean an ear to sound. I'd close my eyes for filling, follow the strings of music, and slip down into its colors. All other sounds faded. My body, rain rhythm, and the music became all. After awhile I could make a poem and slide back into the downpour, happy in its beat. I felt special in the rainsong and slow walk home.

One afternoon as I wandered the aisles, a slim creamed-skinned lady with rouge-circled cheeks motioned to me. As she crooked her finger, my first thought was to apologize for entering this secret world supposed to be for adults. Yet she didn't seem really threatening. Cautiously, I went toward the woman, noting the gray day through the window framing her pale hazel hair and the openness of her arms held still at either side of herself. She smelled of softness as she asked, "Would you like to have a booth for yourself?"

Magic!

The only thing I could say was, "I can't buy no music!"

A soft smile spread as she slowly shook her head asking, "No? Well, can you listen anyway?"

I jiggled an affirmative head. She said, "I'm Mrs. Smith, and this is my store so you're welcome here anytime."

Feeling drained away from my body as she took the tips of my fingers to lead me to a listening booth. There were no words as she bent toward me, asking, "Is there something special you'd like to hear?"

"No, Ma'am," staggered out, but Mrs. Smith, undaunted by my lacking, said, "Well, you wait here. I'll come back with something wonderful."

I wanted to run, but my legs weighed too heavy. An adult approached the booth, saying, "Oh, excuse me," just as though I belonged. I slid to floor, sitting down as I wrested my folded spiral binder from my back pocket and my pencil from above my ear where writers always carried them. Mrs. Smith returned to my show of calm confidence and put on *Peter and the Wolf*. Story and music!

How could she have known? Grownups usually didn't understand about such things. They often forgot their heart secrets. But the days that followed, where I could pick anything I wanted to listen to, proved me wrong. Billie Holiday sang sadness after I'd listen to tribal music and wonder where my father was. Big Band sounds signaled tears of missing mother, but Scott Joplin had a "Maple Leaf Rag" that warmed. Beethoven got mad and made thunderous rain. Haydn knew the calm of a sunny Lake Washington.

Mrs. Smith asked what I was writing as though it were really important and not merely an adult being tolerant. She let me read her poem after poem without laughing or correcting the English or telling me not to dream. She'd say, "You keep doing that," and patted my head. I'd leave the music store with the feeling of being cuddled in sunlight, even in the rain. It was really quite all right to be a cross-eyed funny Indian kid who secretly scribbled poetry. Mrs. Smith said it was good. And all those different people of all those colors and looks on all those records knew it was too.

Many years later, when I was forty-five and in a cold early-spring-drizzle mood, I went into Standard Records and Hi-Fi feeling the need for some new music to match the time I wanted to spend writing. In one of the floorworn aisles still narrow with record bins, I stopped for the passage of an Elder. Her thin body, shoulder-stooped and year-wrinkled, slipped sprightly past me. She smiled at my having slightly bowed with hand gesturing for her to have right of way. A warm rush flooded over me. I watched her bending toward a customer, her slight hands softly bridging the width of a record as she placed it on a turntable. She had not been in the store the other times I had come since growing up. I waited until she was behind the counter again, then stood before her, feeling shy.

Mrs. Smith asked me if there was anything else I wanted other than the Billie Holiday I'd chosen. I took in deep air and said, "I want to thank you for all the times you listened to my poetry as a kid and for your patting my head."

A puzzled face turned up toward me, a broad smile cresting her mouth. I told her about her gift. She grinned more widely and said, "How nice that I could be there for you to save some beauty. The world needs people like you in it. Well, I'll pat your head again."

GLEN SIMPSON

"I was born at Atlin, British Columbia, on October 9, 1941. My father's side of the family includes Tahltan and Kaska Athabaskans from the area of the Stikine and upper Dease rivers. I graduated with an M.F.A. in metals from R.I.T.s School for American Craftsmen in 1969 and since then have been teaching at the University of Alaska, Fairbanks.

"'Respect' is the word most commonly used by older Athabaskans in describing their view of the world, respect not only for people, as in the Christian concept of 'do unto others . . . ,' but for every element of nature whether animate or inanimate. Our perception is shaped by our fundamental beliefs: when I search deeply within myself I often come up with imagery based on an Athabaskan perspective."

FRONT STREET

Front street Nome,
where cultures meet in the mud:
hunters,
whose eyes swept the horizon,
search in a thickening fog,
lost on the drifting ice of an unknown sea
while foraging for one more beer.
Sons of farmers,
seeking what they couldn't find at home,
seek even harder
as they step too heavily
on this last thin edge of America.

Who can tell them
that they are formed in the image of angels?

YUKON RIVER

Padding kayak in the cold of night
the river spirits rise
the body shrinks
rhythm drives me on.
I see a weeping woman floating there
and wonder:
does she cry for both of us,
or rivers past, or rivers yet to come?

STICK DANCE, NULATO

The urge to silence penetrated every corner,
every child, every rambling drunk.
"Don't look back" said a clear voice,
a woman old enough to tell them of their place;
take only the Spirits of the dead,
is what she really meant.

The door was opened.
Cold fog danced there,
pushing against the breath of men,
rushing out and wrapping each chosen dresser
as they met the night.
All doubt was frozen in that instant
when the Spirits said their last goodbye.

OVERNIGHT AT BOUNDARY HOUSE, 1984

I awoke in the darkness of that great hollow house.
An outboard peaked and went on
into the depths of night.
Heart and lungs picked up the beat
as my grandparents returned to that space:
young and strong they walked about.
Bread was baking, sled dogs chafed on their chains
out there in the rich coastal grass.
For one bright unhurried moment
I looked in on the zenith of their lives.

I dared to move and it was gone;
the screen door hung askew,
the windows fly specked and stuffed with rags.
A pack rat searched like a thief in the back room.
Tomorrow night I would sleep in the tent.

STEAMERS ON THE YUKON, 1944

Red paddle wheels beat the snow melt water
like a dying whale.
We stood on clay banks yielding to each surge:
waves marching to a coal fired metronome.
Wood cutter's kids we were
dwarfed like the bank swallows dipping overhead.

THE SHAMAN'S WORDS

I reached for his words in that place
so thick with people and their sounds;
"In those days the women flowered
with the cycle of the moon," he said.
Flowered!
I saw the salt tide thrashing at its peak,
as his truth washed over me.

R. A. SWANSON

R. A. "Bob" Swanson, a writer who makes his home in Yakima, Washington, is Ojibwe from the Grand Portage Reservation in northeastern Minnesota. Swanson's writings, which have been published for the past twenty years, carry the message that it's all right to be an Indian, and that people are all the same no matter what color the skin.

His works have been published in anthologies in the United States and Canada, in magazines on the West Coast and in New York, New Mexico, Alaska, and Oklahoma. He has published eight books of his writings, and his most recent book, *Breaking Stereotypes*, was published in Poland in 1986. He has also recently completed an audio tape entitled "Drummers, Dancers, and Singers."

AN OLD MAN ASKS

where are the young men
the strength
of my village

you took them to town
to become gamblers and drunks

where are the young women
the beauty
of my village

you took them to town
to become barmaids and dancers

where are the children
the pride
of my village

you took them to town
to be left at the movies

i am alone the strength
the beauty the pride the last
of my village

i ask you now
where are you taking me

TWO SISTERS

we need food!
You give us food?

Have you gotten food
from us in the
last ninety days?

no
we was to come here
last months
but we never had
money for gas.

Do you have money
for gas now?

yes

Why didn't you
spend it for food?

THE DRUMS TOUCH

Drum beats
Heart beats
Hoof beats
Drum beat meets
Heart beat

Vibrations tell all
Listen
To the heart beat
Listen
To the hoof beat

Drums touch brings
The sound of
Skin on skin
Stretched over cedar
Stretched over bone

Hoof beat
Heart beat
Drum beat
Blend into

One

Hoof beats give life
To become drumbeats
Drumbeats bring life
To the
Heart

WE ARE ALL WARRIORS

We are all warriors
doing battle every day
We prove ourselves in combat
fighting in different ways

We are fighting for rights
and recognition
We are fighting for respect
and understanding

We battle for acceptance
individually
We battle for respect
as a nation

We fight with ourselves
and each other
We are all warriors
doing battle every day

THE WANDERER'S PRAYER

mother of the mountains
father of the skies
guide me in my travels
be with me when I die

brother of the forests
sister of the streams
protect me in my travels
be with me in my dreams

[Untitled]

When the spirit moves you
go up on top of the mountain
and ask the creator
what should be done for him

when the spirit moves you
strip yourself of all your worldliness
and go up naked
on to the top of the mountain

when the spirit moves you
do as he commands
for his is the voice of the creator
and his life is in your hands

MARY TALLMOUNTAIN

Mary TallMountain is of Koyukon Athabascan Russian Celtic origin, born in Alaska Territory on the Yukon River in 1918. She is a long-time resident of San Francisco, California.

Her work is found in anthologies of the Native American writing community, including *Earth Power Coming*, *The Remembered Earth*, *That's What She Said*, and *Songs From This Earth on Turtle's Back*. Her first collection of poems, *There is No Word for Goodbye*, was printed by the Blue Cloud Quarterly Press; in 1988 *Continuum II* was published as the final volume in the Blue Cloud series of chapbooks.

She writes from an Indian viewpoint about the land and people where she was born, using fiction and poetry. Much of her work is devoted to social justice and societal problems, and can be found in such magazines as *Animals' Agenda* and *Alaska Quarterly*. She was professed a secular Franciscan in 1969 and presently writes a column entitled "Meditations for Wayfarers" in *Way*, a Franciscan publication. She is currently at work on a novel which is set in Alaska.

UNTITLED POEM

Last night you read poems
about trumpet vines and tamarack
in Laguna Pueblo—
a purple dawn twenty years ago.
I know.
There's a place in my mind
filled with sea wind,
deep in Oregon dogwood, lupine,
freckled with wild strawberries.

You rode on a wagon,
pigtails flying,
brown in your treetop jeans.
We rode the Tillamook highway
our '28 Nash chugged, hissed
on the skinny beach road.
Sitting still, I hear again
the horn go ooo-gah!
just before the curve.

You told how light
curled around the haunch of mesa.
Mauve, violet shadows
crept across Haystack Rock,
sunlight sidled into cracks of
the cabin's rough wall,
needled the windowblind.
Invited me, sleepyhead, out
to the dawn and sea.

You remembered wind
beating the horns of mesa.
In coveralls I crawled
onto the highest dune.
Ocean lay long, lazy, gentle,
drumming the shore,

telling the wind there's magic
just beyond the headland.
I still walk to her beat and strum.

In your dreams the sea of sand
poured over ancient rock.
My sand took turns;
gritty and hot; wet and cold.
Sun drove heat
through my small tough soles,
the sand muttered and squeaked
against my flying heels.

Where are they now,
the fires of seadrift,
clashing pans of supper,
the calling voices?
The amber dune beyond the spruces,
where has it drifted?
Rampant, it called to us,
we bellied down on its back,
slithered to the beach.

Last night I saw your mesa,
sea of drifting stone; you
showed the weave of things,
their congruence; that
from our sphere
all ripens into untold time,
unimagined completion.

KOYUKONS HEADING HOME

Laid back on my bed-roll I
Squint up into the sun.
Little mountains are saying spring.
Under my brown desert skin
My old wanderblood knows
How it'll be in May to ride
The ferryboat Columbia
Chugging the inside passage north.

Midnight at Skagway
Hulking in yellow oilskins
First mate bosses the crew
Winching her in. Wooden pilings
Squall in protest.
Lonesome lights shine in the tide.
Fish . . . salt . . . harbor mist . . .
Stick fresh to my face . . .

Saturday night the tourists jump
To get rock music of Silver Plum,
Get up late for Sunday brunch.
Tadpole tails of trawlers
Zip under scowling peaks.
Eagle gauges the exact second
He'll dive to spear
A single flashing salmon.

Morning kids get down around
A cassette tape. A dozen
Black eyes zero in on unseen
Thudding drums of Herbie Vent.
Just one glance
And I know they're
Koyukons too,
Heading home.

GAAL* COMES UPRIVER

Deep in the Bering Sea
Gaal flicks her heavy tail.
Majestic with her mates,
Enters the Yukon tides
Swimming steady north
To the place of Midnight Sun.

Strong in the brown river
She cleaves the miles.
Her fearless eyes
Know swoop and nip of gulls,
Menace of rolling logs,
Black waiting shapes of Bear.

With one compulsion
She will not feed again
On the ancient pilgrimage
To the tiny creek of spawning
Only her genes remember.

In the immense ponder of noon
She rests with the others,
Crimson shadows lying still
Behind the overhang
Of a bank far from the
Icy sea, their home.

Out they stream.
Hidden nets rise to catch.
Gaal flashes wild,
Rosy silver, she arrows
Above hunched backs,
Falls into the circle.

**Gaal* is the Athabascan Indian word for King Salmon, who start the spawning flight from the Bering Sea to the Yukon River in early May.

The net tautens.
She hangs to it, thrashes,
Shoots to the surface,
Lunges, arches, flutters
Away from the churning mass,
Above dismay and gaping jaws.

Gaal jackknifes free,
Sweeps on upriver.

THE SPY'S NEST

for my brother Bill

Under the dark and huddled hill,
Broken windows wink at the sun.
The house I thought giant-sized
Crouches small and gray, its
Weathered walls beaten to silver
By cat-o'-nine-tailed
Polar winds.

Fat blue festoons of delphinium
Blow beyond the broken gate.
Scent of sweet alyssum fades
In the brass crucible of noon.
We crouch under bending reeds
In our green and secret cave—
The spy's nest on the riverbank.

Around the sawhorse in the yard
Yellow dust piled high
And the little pails thrown down.
The swing dangles lonely.
Children's voices, high and thin,
Shout from the alder grove,
Far away as the stars.

Grizzled old malamute Moose
Twitches, dreaming in the red wagon,
Runs the Iditarod Race.*
Suddenly he bounds awake,
Barks me home, soundless.
I almost cry his name
Into the quiet breast of summer.

*Historical Alaskan winter cross-country race.

EARLE THOMPSON

"Sometimes, I do not know if I will ever learn how I came to be a writer ..., born in Nespelem, Washington, on March 13, 1950, growing up and living on the Yakima Indian Reservation which is located in the southcentral portion of Washington state. Obviously my roots lie in the oral tradition that I learned from my grandfather. Often when I sit at the writing table, my grandfather materializes and walks off the page becoming real. Grandfather relates the story of creation; I listen and I watch the animal people roaming and trying to understand their young world. Through my writing, I try to grasp and express this magic—the delicate balance and our responsibility to care for the earth and each other."

Earle's work has been included in a number of anthologies including *Harper's Anthology of 20th Century Native American Poets* (Harper & Row), *Anthology of Third World Writing* (Pig Iron Press), and *Songs of This Earth on Turtle's Back* (Greenfield Review Press). He has also published work in a number of magazines including *Akewon, AtlAtl, Argus, Blue Cloud Quarterly, Contact II, Greenfield Review, Northwest Arts, Northwest Indian News, The Portland Review, Prison Writing Review*, and *The Wicazo Sa Review*. His collection of poetry, *The Juniper Moon Pulls At My Bones* was published in 1985 by the Blue Cloud Quarterly Press (vol. 32, no. 2) and won the "Written Arts" Competition in the annual Bumbershoot Literary Arts festival in Seattle, Washington.

VIGIL

I dip my net and the wooden pole
with its metal rim shivers.

The sky is still
as a salmon flutters upward
in the foaming water.
In midriver, salmon and water
merge on an ancient plane,
becoming momentarily
white.

The Columbia moves and swells
then spreads itself out
becoming a calm blue in my vision.

Celilo Falls'* voice is a soft breeze
nestled in bleached bones
and haunting sagebrush
along the shore.

*Celilo Falls on the Columbia River was an important ancient fishing ground for Indians from all over the Northwest. They continued to fish and hold ceremonial gatherings until the Falls was completely covered by a dam constructed in 1956 by the Army Corps of Engineers.

DESIGN IN BLUE

She conceives a blue appaloosa
on the beige canvas backing,
making preparations to bead a purse.
Hawk screeches; children
play in the morning. She turns,
watches them, causing her to lose
count of her shiny-cut beads.

She rises from the August grass
and her children in the meadow,
the boys discard the entrails
of a freshly killed pheasant
into the stream as they were taught.
The water is bright and red, clouding
swirling, it becomes clear again.

She waxes and threads the needle,
and she begins to bead, looping around
through four blue beads
and ties them down. She smiles
and continues to bead,
listening to the galloping hooves
of the blue appaloosa in the meadow.

SHE WALKS IN NEW-BORN LEAVES

as she walks her long hair is a raven
in flight with the August breeze;
dark strands appear to lash the blue.

I am ensnared, and her skin
becomes stars and glistens
in the fragile moonlight.

Sleeping, she dreams
of designs on the basket
for when the huckleberries ripen.

How she moves along the path
and with her rustlings the earth
becomes adorned with new-born leaves.

AFTERNOON VIGIL

Dust from the gravel road settles
and tints the mint field.

She stands scaling salmon,
while glistening flakes fall
becoming stars on the earth.

Magpie watches as a breeze nestles
among the braided ears of corn draped
over a pole in the shed.

She brushes a strand of hair
away from her face and continues
working at the wooden table.

Sun warms and colors the salmon flesh
and magpie laughs into the afternoon.

SPIRIT

Salmon leaps into fine mist and the old scaffolds
shiver, the structures protrude from the rocky shore.
My sore hands grasp the braided metal,
and I watch fishermen dip their long poles, the bone-
colored nets skim the water. The drifting aroma
of fish permeates the cable car as we sway in the wind.

I unload glistening salmon, feeling the stickiness
and wipe it on my jeans and the corners
of the wooden box. The smell of dried blood.
Flies circle, I try swatting them,
beads of perspiration stream down my face,
neck and chest.

Perspiration and blood, it creates a membrane.
The film fragments and I can almost peel it

from my skin. Salmon slide and the ice becomes smudged.
Stark eyes stare, eyes at jutting angles
glare and I hook one through the eye
and throw it in the long, rectangular box.

I don't consider them dead, even though I clubbed
their heads with a sawed-off bat. And I don't feel
as though I am killing them. They are food.
I watch as their shiny bodies wriggle, arch and dance
on the earth. I feel their spirit. I pray, I sing
and dance for them. We understand each other.

WHALE SONG

"My brother, let me hear you sing,
Feel the sunlight on your moist fin."

Speelyi spoke adjusting his medicine belt,
his long, dark hair glistening in the spring.

Bleached bones gather sound and seagulls twist
and plunge graying the edges of the ancient rocks.

Speelyi, the Trickster, roams the young world
watching the salmon return from the sea.

On the shore, he carves cedar into a whale
and feels the smoothness of the abalone fin inlay.

Whale joyously surfaces, its arc becoming blue.
"Yes, my Brother, I watch you emerging.

My Brother, let me hear your voice,
Let me listen and learn your song."

DANCER

Coyote dances a jig on the edge of the world.
Mist clinging to his long hair and orange skies
with blackberry stains darkening the earth.

"E nou e shun ă?" Coyote asks squatting by the fire.
"Chow, no, I do not want to eat," I answer him.
"Well, brud-ur. Wanna hear a good story, boy?"
"Yes, Speelyi."

The appaloosa's mane shivers, its ebony flanks
speckled with white resembling stars
against a darkened sky;
Round brown eyes become evening crickets
chirping in the sweet grass.

"Son, let me spout sum poetry,
As yellow beads drift through morning cedar.
The color of honey becoming freckles
on her breasts that I can almost taste . . ."

"Whoa, slow down. I hope you're not speaking to me.
But what does this mean?" I query.

"No, no . . . 'au contraire' pard. Me heart
she is broken, she will not have anything to do with me.
I chased after her, promising her gifts and powers.
Still, she won't bother with me because she loves
another. Again, I promise her
that she will forget. She cries, and I feel sad
for her. I cannot destroy her or even trick her.
And I have tried, but that is another story, my friend.
So, for others to know her beauty—I made her
into a waterfall. You can feel her mist touching
your face and you can understand her beauty.
Do you follow me?" Speelyi smiles tending the fire.

"No, not really." I reply, knowing now why
he is called the Trickster.

Whippoorwill ruffles its gray feathers,
it scurries into the blush of blue lingering
like a veil on the meadow.

Again, Coyote begins dancing on the rim of the world
and the angle of geese shifts on the evening skyline.

GAIL TREMBLAY

Gail Tremblay is a writer of Onondaga, MicMac and French Canadian origin who was born in Buffalo, New York. For the past eight years she has lived and taught in Washington state and has been actively involved in the Native American arts community in the Northwest. She has published poems in *Denver Quarterly, Calyx, Northwest Review*, and *Maize*. Her work has been anthologized in *The Anthology of Magazine Verse and Yearbook of American Poets, A Nation Within, Sandhills and Other Geographies, The Harper's Anthology of Native American Poetry*, and *Voices from the Longhouse*. Her book-length collection of poetry, *Talking to the Grandfathers*, is published in *Annex 21*, no. 3, by the University of Nebraska at Omaha.

Calyx Press (Corvallis, Oregon) published her book of poems, *Indian Singing in Twentieth Century America*, in January 1990.

COYOTE, HANGING IN A MUSEUM, COMES OFF THE WALL

(for Harry Fonseca)

After days of blue haired ladies commenting
on the odd slant of your eyes, asking
if real men wear earrings, or, "darling
perhaps he's supposed to be a pirate";
after hearing, "my what big teeth
you have," as if all people's stories
are the same, Coyote gets lonely
for brown women whose grandfathers
told them tales, whose memories
collect adventures that run deep in time
when everything was changeable.
Coyote waits 'til no one is looking,
comes off the wall to check out other
rooms. Hoping he's found the girl
of his dreams, ripe and ready,
he laps the ass of a Maillol bronze
and sniffs the air. The hard, cold surface
caresses no one's tongue, makes him
wish for desert girls who sing
while they grind corn, who know they own
the world and shyly catch the image
of a stare in the corners of their eyes.
How was it that he ever let that bright-eyed,
brown man with the wild hair talk him
into posing, tell him fame would make them
both rich; one has to laugh, mangy gambler;
one has to laugh at where vanity and wealth
will take one. An Indian understands
you're just a horny devil playing tricks
on yourself and making the whole world
rich with ironies while people try to figure
out what the image you're creating means.

THE RETURNING

It is these long journeys to the heart
of the continent, moving too fast
thirty thousand feet above the planet
that leave me longing to whisper
to medicine roots that send shoots
as fine as hair for miles to anchor
themselves to ground. The body feels
strangely out of context. I desire
to see agates sparkle among cirrus clouds
stretched out like endless waves
washing no shore. I grow lonely
for the dirt, lonely for the horizon
that marks time in relation to sun
and stars as it spins across the sky.
Up here, there are momentary miracles:
outside Denver, a lake turns golden
as it mirrors sun; clouds and mountains
move together creating atmosphere
for one another as Earth arcs through space.
But this journey is a pause in normal
breathing; a movement through thin air
kept away by delicate walls and will,
this distant place is not meant to sustain
the flesh. Even birds fly miles
below knowing the plants creating
air can only send their life giving
gift so far. It is the returning to Earth
that lets the skin contain the pulse,
the returning to Earth that feeds the muscle
of the heart and makes love possible.

IT IS IMPORTANT

On dark nights, when thoughts fly like nightbirds
looking for prey, it is important to remember
to bless with names every creature that comes
to mind; to sing a thankful song and hold
the magic of the whole creation close in the heart,
to watch light dance and know the sacred is alive.
On dark nights, when owls watch, their eyes
gleaming in the black expanse of starless sky,
it is important to gather the medicine bones,
the eagle feathers, the tobacco bundles, the braided
sweetgrass, the cedar, and the sage, and pray
the world will heal and breath feed the plants
that care for the nations keeping the circle whole.
On dark nights, when those who think only of themselves
conjure over stones and sing spells to feed their wills,
it is important to give gifts and to love everything
that shows itself as good. It is time to turn
to the Great Mystery and know the Grandfathers have
mercy on us that we may help the people to survive.
On dark nights, when confusion makes those who envy
hate and curse the winds, face the four directions
and mumble names, it is important to stand
and see that our only work is to give what others
need, that everything that touches us is a holy
gift to teach us we are loved. When sun rises,
and light surrounds life making blessings grow,
it is important to praise its coming, and exhale
letting all we hold inside our lungs travel east
and mix its power with the air; it is important to praise
dawn's power breathing in and know we live in good
relation to all creation and sing what must be sung.

LIGHT SHAKES

Light shakes among waves, reflects
off facets cut in fluid by the wind.
The surface rocks and fish leap
and dive into a weedy world
that breathes through gills
as startling as the plumes
of egrets gown inside chambers
of flesh covered with scales. Dark
among rocks, sand dollars bristle
and know light lines as delicate
as threads wound and bound in lace,
light sinking from the surface
of the Sound to create elaborate
patterns on the sand. This world
spins between continents careening
through the stars, a chariot to rock
us in our dreams and teach us
how to bear the pain of being
only human in bodies so momentary
that our bones grow naked before all
our love is spent and gone away.

VINCE WANNASSAY

Vincent Wannassay was born in Pendleton, Oregon, and is of the Umatilla tribe who are located in eastern Oregon.

He attended the Institute of American Indian Arts at Santa Fe, New Mexico where he received his Associate of Fine Arts degree. He also has a Bachelor of Arts degree from the College of Santa Fe.

While at I.A.I.A., he studied creative writing under the tutelage of Joy Harjo, the noted Native American writer. He was co-editor of the "Spearhead Press," the I.A.I.A. school paper and was a member of the school's writers' club, The Red Earth Writers. His work has been anthologized in *Rolling Thunder, Voice of the People*.

Vincent is presently living in Portland, Oregon. He is a charter member of the Northwest Native Writers group. Vince is working on a series of short stories dealing with the plight of urban Indians in a Northwest city.

MURDER ON THE TRI-MET

I was riding on the bus

one sunny day
I saw a bee, flying around
in the bus.

He didn't pay . . .
He got killed by a little ole lady
who did . . .

OBSERVATIONS

There was a small

Viking ship
sailing across a New Mexico sidewalk
one sunny day

I looked again

It was only a shadow
of an Ant

carrying a piece of grass

BROKEN TRADITION

As I walked through the park one day
I saw a young man sitting on the grass
beside a tree, playing a guitar.

A dead squirrel lay beside him.
I walked up to him, looked at the squirrel
"What happened?" I asked the young man.
He looked at me.

"I don't know," he said.
"I was just sitting here, playing my guitar,
and . . . plop!
and squirrel's laying there . . . dead beside me."

I looked around the park.
I watched the other squirrels.
This is what I surmised.
Squirrel had broken "TRADITION".

Instead of hunting for berries and nuts,
he went begging for "junk food"
Candy, popcorn etc.
he was showing off.

He climbed up too high in the tree,
got sick, fell out of the tree.
Broke his neck . . .
"Tsk-tsk . . . Brother Squirrel"

Shoulda stuck to Tradition.

TREATIES

I believe

that

U.S. Government . . . Native American . . . treaties
are made on "Mental Reservations"

A Catholic priest told me
in Religion class
A "Mental Reservation" is a
"little white lie"

HIGHER POWER

MONEY
is my higher power

I'm an atheist this week
I'm broke . . .

JAMES WELCH

Of Blackfoot/Gros-Ventre heritage, James Welch is an internationally acclaimed poet and novelist. His first publication, a collection of poems entitled *Riding the Earthboy 40* was published by Harper & Row in 1971. His well-known novels include *Winter In the Blood* (Harper & Row 1974), *The Death of Jim Loney* (Harper & Row 1979), and the widely acclaimed historical novel of the Blackfeet, *Fool's Crow* (Harper & Row 1987). Jim makes his home in Missoula, Montana, and is currently at work on a new novel.

RIDING THE EARTHBOY 40

Earthboy: so simple his name
should ring a bell for sinners.
Beneath the clowny hat, his eyes
so shot the children called him
dirt, Earthboy farmed this land
and farmed the sky with words.

The dirt is dead. Gone to seed
his rows becoming marker to a grave
vast as anything but dirt.
Bones should never tell a story
to a bad beginner. I ride
romantic to those words,

those foolish claims that he
was better than dirt, or rain
that bleached his cabin
white as bone. Scattered in the wind
Earthboy calls me from my dream:
Dirt is where the dreams must end.

CHRISTMAS COMES TO MOCCASIN FLAT

Christmas comes like this: Wise men
unhurried, candles bought on credit (poor price
for calves), warriors face down in wine sleep.
Winds cheat to pull heat from smoke.

Friends sit in chinked cabins, stare out
plastic windows and wait for commodities.
Charlie Blackbird, twenty miles from church
and bar, stabs his fire with flint.

When drunks drain radiators for love
or need, chiefs eat snow and talk of change,

an urge to laugh pounding their ribs.
Elk play games in high country.

Medicine Woman, clay pipe and twist tobacco,
calls each blizzard by name and predicts
five o'clock by spitting at her television.
Children lean into her breath to beg a story:

Something about honor and passion,
warriors back with meat and song,
a peculiar evening star, quick vision of birth.
Blackbird feeds his fire. Outside, a quick 30 below.

THE ONLY BAR IN DIXON

These Indians once imitated life.
Whatever made them warm
they called wine, song or sleep,
a lucky number on the tribal roll.

Now the stores have gone the gray
of this November sky. Cars
whistle by, chrome wind, knowing
something lethal in the dust.

A man could build a reputation here.
Take that redhead at the bar—
She knows we're thugs, killers
on a fishing trip with luck.

No luck. No room for those
sensitive enough to know they're beat.
Even the Flathead turns away,
a river thick with bodies,

Indians on their way to Canada.
Take the redhead—yours for just a word,
a promise that the wind will warm
and all the saints come back for laughs.

THANKSGIVING AT SNAKE BUTTE

In time we rode that trail
up a butte as far as time
would let us. The answer to our time
lay hidden in the long grasses
on the top. Antelope scattered

through the rocks before us, clattered
unseen down the easy slope to the west.
Our horses balked, stiff-legged,
their nostrils flared at something unseen
gliding smoothly through brush away.

On top, our horses broke, loped through
a small stand of stunted pine, then jolted
to a nervous walk. Before us lay
the smooth stones of our ancestors, the fish,
the lizard, snake and bent-kneed

bowman—etched by something crude,
by a wandering race, driven by their names
for time: its winds, its rain, its snow
and the cold moon tugging at the crude figures
in this, the season of their loss.

DAVID WHITED

David Lloyd Whited has published several volumes of poetry including *Hollow Fox* and, most recently, *The Fire's Purpose* (Burnaby, British Columbia: Cowan & Tetley Press, 1987). David obtained his B.A. in English and mathematics from Southern Oregon State College and earned his M.F.A. in poetry from Bowling Green State University in 1976. Since that time he has been working as a planner and grantwriter for Indian health program development. Currently he is the health planner for the Puyallup Tribal Health Authority. He has co-authored numerous articles on Indian mental health care.

David was born and raised in Oregon. Although he is of Flathead ancestry, David has never been to the home reservation on the Flathead. He was raised among the Cow Creek Umpqua people and the Klamath people in the Umpqua Valley in Oregon.

DAMN MOON; SHE'S A HARD ONE!

Weaving and threading things, we make this life we wear.
I have been close enough to the edge to feel the vacuum.
To understand that out here, when you cry out
there are no echoes. Touch the leaf
& the tree trembles. It is history.
Serenity is possible in stones.
But it is hard to walk & be serene.
Hard to hold the sky in your eyes.
I have tried too hard to stop the wind
though the moon arcs clear.

It's strange how endings turn you to beginnings.
This rain here has begun. lightning
& thunder pitch & roll across the sound.
I wake from a close strike
the light still shaking in my eyes.
soft hands have left bruises green blue & tender.
all these pyramids of past hands
the empty circle of my arms:
this is a geometry past thirty & alone
among parallel lines. There's a fever of tiny moths
& electric lights in this raining fall.
They turn, drawing down the moon with their dancing.

BLENDING WIND & STONES

It is a need she has identified
like the slow winter and cold wind
the stones shall be bent to the wind
& like leaves don't mind the dying
knowing too well that all seasons cut the heart.
I rock here in my white walled apartment
I rock and sway here alone to this music.
today, there's just no time to look out the window.

stone wind cuts the heart. it is simple.
easier to blend wind and cold stars/wind & light
it is easier to remember only the light things
only the bright moments & that bright flash
when most things fall together blending
wind & stones, the motion of each, and we sing:

this is how the darkness grows
& this is how the darkness knows
what to find & when to find you there.
(stone to bone. wind to breath.)
this is how the darkness moves
& this is what the darkness makes you lose
what you want & when you want it there.
(stone to flesh.   breath to breath.)
this is what the darkness knows
& this is what the darkness knows how to find
& why you need the darkness there.
(stone to wind.   breath to breath.)
this is why the darkness lingers
& half the world knows darkness always
& what to cover, what to hide from light.
(windstone.   windbone.   fleshbreath.)
this is how the darkness finds its way
& this is why the darkness will not stay
we move through darkness.   it does not move through us.
we blend wind & stones.   minds to hearts to rest.
this is what we claim the darkness knows
& this is how we claim the darkness moves
though it is our catching light which makes the dark.
(breath to breath.   wind to light.   stone to heart.)

EMPTY RATS IN THE CUPBOARD

These are skinny times.
thin like flint. Basalt flaked fine
into a hunting point. rubbing the trail
for any fresh sign.

we have a stiff need for more sky
for an empty space somewhere
which is ours alone to fill.
trotting this fresh crust of trail
through the meadow.

scatter those bones: this is the skull
left empty & pale but unbroken.
There is no way to keep the wildness
out/the animal in.

something paces beyond the garden fence/
beyond the nettle hedge.
See how the prints rest.
how the air stiffens them.
how we trace the edge of grass
our eyes this close to the ground.

Nothing here will eat out of your hands.
Nothing ever would eat out of mine.

[Untitled]

The Modoc kind of remind me of the Nez Perce
in their friendliness.
You know, Captain Jack's father told him
"you have to learn the white man's ways
& get along with them. you have to try."
because he foresaw what would happen.
& he knew.
& Captain Jack tried like hell.

They used to go right into Shasta and trade.
all the way over to the coast.
& his father died when they poisoned all them
people—gave them those blankets, you know,
full of sickness.   poison food.   & they died.
Nobody knows how many of them.
because they were friendly & tried to get along.
eager to learn, they accepted.
& Captain Jack tried.

Even that didn't quite do it.
because it was such a strange dying.
he just couldn't quite understand.
& Captain Jack did try to understand.
he finally asked only that the people could live
in the lava beds.   among the rocks.
& that is finally where he was forced to run.

RAMONA WILSON

Ramona Wilson is a member of the Colville Confederated Tribes. She was born in Nespelem, Washington, and lived in the Monse area until she was sixteen. She is now a teacher and currently is a Project Director for an American Indian Bilingual Program in the Oakland, California, public schools.

She has been publishing her material since the age of seventeen. She has this to say about her writing: "I have had many things and events, many people and many other writers, both Indian and non-Indian, influence me and my writing. But always, and more each day, I am influenced by place, the land under and around everything. Always in my mind is the first country and the first people I ever came to know. This is the connection I need to make a poem."

PASSING BATTLEFIELDS

It was still winter.
We had no place in common
that waited for us, other towns
lay on our shoulders, mirrored
our eyes, as we looked down
over the brown hill and imagined horses
stiff legged, soft dust stopped noses
trembling for the smell of water,
their riders a weight of metal and sweat,
as they half-fell towards the wild rose
and willow scented canyon.

The battles here are not marked.
The few people had little cover,
the far hills were dreams.
They had brown skin and names
whispered into the air
that sounded like earth and birds.
Winds took the cries
that rose like the echoes
they already were,
and swallowed them, a great
and finally merciful thing.

There is no place we can go
nowhere to be a tourist
nowhere we are ever anonymous.
The histories of the creeks,
of ravines that don't go through
welcome us, we visit awhile.

We are the children that were to come
when the world would be changed.
So they said it would happen.

SPOKANE MUSEUM

These are not relics
from lost people, lost lands.
I know where they are.
Give me that digging tool.
I'll show you where
in the spring we get roots.
The wind will come, as it does,
blowing our dresses and hair
as we bend with certainty,
the pink flowers in our hands,
the earth dropping
through our fingers.

DECEMBER ON THE COAST

As I sleep the Grey Whales
swim and blow a smell of green and sea
into the moon-cold air.
They do not sleep, they court
and play even as they pull south
to the lagoons and sky
some have never seen.

All things fall away
before their intentness
their bulk rising like prophecy,
like dreams that begin
the same way, time after time.
They have no count
of miles or years
but answer to a memory
that is its own need.

I turn over with a dream of sun
turning my sleep like waves.
I wake restless into a day
murmuring of migrations.

SECOND GOODBYE FOR SUE

On the freeway, Van on the radio
the morning is driving itself
towards the west and me with it,
stepping on the gas of the world.
I remember how you travelled,
loved to go, didn't matter where
it was the moving that was the pleasure,
the kick that would light your eyes
and I remember the parties
dancing until the first bird woke
in the trees already luminescent
as we said goodnight at the step
the houses lying about us, mute and stupid.

We would embrace, still laughing,
our hair long and young,
blowing from the wind in the roads
we couldn't wait to get on.

ELIZABETH WOODY

Elizabeth Woody is a Warm Springs, Wasco/Navajo Indian. She majored in creative writing at the Institute of American Indian Arts in Santa Fe, New Mexico. Her work has been widely anthologized, and publications include national and international magazines. *Hand Into Stone*, her first volume of poetry, was published in 1988 by Contact II Press. Her poems have appeared in *Songs From This Earth on Turtle's Back, The Clouds Threw This Light, A Gathering of Spirit, Bearing Witness/Sobreviviendo, The Native American Today, Fireweed, Tyuonyi, Akewon, Contact II, Greenfield Review*, and *Sur Le Dos La Torture: Revue Bilingue de Litterature Amerindienne* (France). In 1985 she won a poetry contest and was published along with seventeen other poets in *Image*, a project of the Seattle Arts Commission. Her work was juried into the Literary Readings series of the National Women's Studies Conference at the University of Washington. Elizabeth currently makes her home in Portland, Oregon.

IN MEMORY OF CROSSING THE COLUMBIA

CONCEPTION

My board and blanket were Navajo,
but my bed is inside the River.
In the beads of remembrance,
I am her body in my father's hands.
She gave me her eyes
and the warmth of basalt.
The vertebrae of her back,
my breastplate, the sturdy
belly of mountainside.

"Pahtu," he whispered in her language.
She is the mountain of change.
She is the mountain of women
who have lain as volcanoes
before men.

Red, as the woman much loved,
she twisted like silvery chinook
beyond his reach.

Dancing the Woman-Salmon dance,
there is not much time to waste.

HAND INTO STONE

In memory of Elizabeth Thompson Pitt, 1908–1987
"Someday the land will be our eyes and skin again."

Her creped fingers,
teethmarked with red speckles,
held mine tight
as she showed our finger moons to me.
They grew together as snowy stones
scratching themselves sleepily.

She had long fingers
with the mobility of spiders.
I felt them at night
as they climbed my skin.
She wrapped us
in tight shells
with agate crystals.

We breathed our own breath
under this cover.

OF STEPS TO DROWNING

The pain of empty flower stems
held the few hairs,
the brightness
that must be recaptured.
Disappearing as strings
of romance, they are resonate as a tight bow
for selected deer.

They wish to wander
under current with lost needs
and fly in moss with conifers.

They hold little stars of dew
in lack of other possessions or petals
for charm, peer into faces
to destination and last mourn.

Hands, burnt bone and dusty,
offer rain caches of gems.
Moving in sign talk for swollen eyes
they reach for voice
to the open cave and rushes of silent bats.
They disappear with small wings.

Beside scented chants
the meadowlark dips vocal
with river and crisp grass.

The wishes reach for gifts
to wandering hair, but are armless
to rub these blind, folded eyes.

As a new buck in itchy velvet,
one rubs to the skin translucent,
tight against the receptacles of light.
The irises are of nights dreaming.

The losses are small sounds of moaning.
Bead necklaces of stone and shell
slide into the world of minnows.
Bones grasp at mosses and branch
to muddy the water for drowning.

ORIGINATING FIRE

For the communities affected by the Hanford Nuclear Reservation

A barren thief scratches at the door
and dims the moon, the candle
to answer inferior medicines.
That empty spirit haunts our origins
tapping our likeness into conformity.

Light on the skyline is First Fire
never leaving its journey, waiting.
There is a movement of foreign substance
rumbling bones into tuffaceous soil.

Boulders and tule huts move without light and sound
away from the impressions basalt formed in the wake
of smoke. Blown into the grunts of animals.
Children sleep through the nightmare,
where the fire uncontrolled fire
is imprisoned light.

WILLIAM S. YELLOW ROBE, JR.

William S. Yellow Robe, Jr., is an enrolled Assiniboine of the Fort Peck Tribes located in northeastern Montana. He and his wife are presently living in Wolf Point, Montana.

William is a writer, playwright, actor, and director. His full-length plays include *Independence of Eddy Rose*, *A Stray Dog*, and a musical, *Harvest*. His one act plays include *Sneaky*, *Wink-dah*, *The Pendleton Blanket*, *The Breaking of Another Circle*, and *Taking Aunty Her Wake*.

He is a member of The Dramatists Guild, Inc., The Northwest Playwrights Guild, and the Minneapolis Playwrights Center.

The Burning of Uncle

The banked gravel road sticks out from the flat land like a scratch on a hand.

Three men are trotting towards the road from across the field. They bob up and down and slowly make their way to the road. Like field mice finding refuge in a sage bush, they go to a small opening into the brush and cottonwood trees that line the road.

"Ho, ho, ho, pretty damn cold," says the larger man. The collar of his long wool coat has four holes cut on each side and the sides are tied together by a leather boot lace like the shank of a high-top tennis shoe. He wipes the small streams of sweat from his forehead and it glistens. A scar from the side of his lip runs to his nose and causes a break in his mustache. He comes to a stop and waits for the other two men. His name is Skiddo.

"Hey, Hey? How come-come-how come-we-we have to run? You'll freeze out our lungs, Skiddo." This man's name is Bull Cookies. He walks around for a moment and comes to a stop and rubs his hump of a belly. A bath towel serves as a cap and earmuffs. He takes off the towel and wipes off the sweat. Then he re-wraps the towel around his head and smiling he looks up into Skiddo's eyes.

"Skiddo, Cah-zin. Why do you want to run for? We're not going to be late for anything." This man's name is Skin. He stays a few feet from the other two men. He bends over and rubs his knees. A tail from his hand-made gopher skin cap snaps down and slaps his eyeglasses. He takes off his glasses and allows the fog to clear from them.

Bull Cookies pats his arms across his own chest and says, "Give him a drink, Skin. He'll warm up boy."

Skin takes out a fifth from underneath his shirt. There are no numbers, letters, or pictures on the bottle. He gives it to Skiddo who unscrews the bottle's cap and drinks. The sucking of the liquid causes his cheeks to pinch. The cap bounces on the crusty snow. "But just one little one hey," says Skin.

"God this one. Getting greedy." Bull Cookies shakes his head. "Is that what they taught you in whiteman's school?"

"No Uncle. They didn't teach me anything." Skin backs away from Bull Cookies and Skiddo. "But I know when I'm cold-hey."

"Never should have sent you off to school. Never should have let you go. Even when that BIA guy threaten to have me thrown in jail." Bull Cookies turns away from Skin. He takes a long draw from the bottle. The bottle's dark green color is shared by the fluid inside, but when a sloppy drink is taken and a drop escapes the grasp of lips the drink is clear like water.

"You know." Bull Cookies walks over to Skin and throws his arm around Skin's shoulder. "I raised this guy here." He kisses Skin. "Right after his father died. His father-my brother."

"He knows you raised me Uncle." Skin is passed the bottle and takes a drink. He looks at Skiddo and takes another drink.

"Good whiskey." Skiddo is bouncing up and down on the balls of his feet. "Better-n' that shit we had before."

"What do you know about good drinking juices? I bet you haven't even tasted your first woman yet-huh." Bull Cookies releases Skin and laughs at Skiddo. "Give me another shot nephew." Bull Cookies tilts the bottle back and causes the alcohol inside the bottle to gurgle.

"Holy-ee, Uncle. Not that thirsty, I hope." Skin takes the bottle and drinks. He then looks at Skiddo and passes it to him. "Here you go Cah-zin."

The sound of the cars on Highway #2 a quarter mile east of them is mingling with the sounds of Skin using a branch to tap on a cottonwood stump. A field mouse watches the three men from a rotted metal bucket. A school bus passes by on the road above them. The bus driver slows the bus down and looks at them. He shakes his head and speeds away and cusses at the three men; the one singing, the one drumming, and the other who is dancing. The bus crawls on the highway that connects Dodson and Oswego, Montana. A farm house a mile south of them comes to life with lights. A cloud hangs over the chimney stack. An owl looks down on the men from atop a cottonwood. The owl raises its wings and hops into the air and slowly glides further down the road. The three men stand a few feet from each other and become the points of a triangle. They pass the bottle. When the bottle is nearly empty the triangle is broken up. Bull Cookies finds a small stump and sits.

"Hey-don't do that." Skiddo is talking to himself and rocks backward on his heels and doesn't look at anyone. He leans forward into the cold. "Cookie. Bull Cookie. Bull-fuck-Cookies. God damn Bull Fuck Cookies."

"What?" Bull Cookies swirls on the stump.

"I'm cold." Skiddo smiles.

"Hey-yeah." Skin agrees and tries to run in place. His ankles get snared by roots and branches of the brush.

"Drink more whiskey, got-damn it. Or-or go home. I think that's what I'm trying to do." Bull Cookies bounces on the stump. "Go home and hide that bottle. They aren't going to catch me, got-damn it."

"Let's go home then." And Skin tightens his grip on the bottle's neck and takes a few steps forward.

"You gonna climb that bank, Skin?" Skiddo looks at Skin and points to the steep gravel bank.

"I thought that guy was bad," Bull Cookies points to Skiddo, "But this guy is worse." Bull Cookies tries to focus on Skiddo. "Go my son-go and get an education-go my son-go and climb a ladder."

"Stop-stop singing that goddamn Mormon song. You goddamn Mormon." Skiddo takes a step towards Bull Cookies. Bull Cookies pinches his nose and blows snot out that leaves a trail on his face. He looks at Skiddo and smiles big.

"Hey-hey-look at my rabbit nose oh-I mean scar," says Bull Cookies. He uses his hand to wipe off the snot and cleans the hand in the two week old snow and dries the hand on a pants leg.

"Goddamn old man. That's disgust-that disgust-its sick-hey." Skiddo charges forward and comes to a sharp halt in front of Bull Cookies. He nearly knocks Bull Cookies over the stump.

"Hey watch it." Bull Cookies leans his head below Skiddo's belly button and clutches Skiddo's hips on the side. Bull Cookies digs his feet into the snow as he tries to steady himself and Skiddo.

"I'm sorry. I'm sorry, Uncle." Skiddo leans over Bull Cookies shoulders. He begins to cry. "Please don't be mad at me, Uncle. I'm sorry. You always treated me good."

"All right, Skiddo. Let go of me got-damn it." Bull Cookies pushes Skiddo, but can't get him off. "All of a sudden I'm everyone's got-damn Uncle."

"Poor Uncle," Skiddo cries harder and claws deeper into Bull Cookies. "He lost his wife."

"Where? Where did you lose her?" Now Skin begins to cry. "I'll go and find her for you, Uncle."

"Stop your crying. Both of you. She's dead. I don't want to talk about it," says Bull Cookies.

Skiddo releases Bull Cookies and steps back. Bull Cookies groans and falls over and passes out.

"He's dead!" Skiddo jumps up and throws both of his arms into the air.

"No! Really?" Skin walks over to Bull Cookies' body. He reaches out with his foot and taps Bull Cookies in the ribs. Bull Cookies moans. "See. He's not dead."

"Oh. I thought he was. Give me a drink," says Skiddo and takes a drink.

"God. I'm cold." Skin runs in place and falls over.

"Hey. Cuzin. Let's build a fire." Skiddo puts the bottle into his coat and goes over to Skin. Skin is trying to get up to his feet and reaches out to Bull Cookies and uses Bull Cookies' body to get up. "Huh-you want to build a fire?"

"No," says Skin.

Skiddo picks up Skin. "Come on. Let's build one."

"No." Skin nearly falls down again.

"Yeah. If we don't, Uncle will freeze. We can use some of these dead branches and I got that paper sack from the bottle," says Skiddo.

"Pull off the dead branches." A small stream of saliva comes to its end on Skin's chin.

Skin and Skiddo gather branches, a few broken fence posts, paper bags and young dead trees. A cock pheasant watches the passing men and is ready for flight. Skin comes too close to the cock and it takes flight from its cover in the brush. Skin runs back to Skiddo. The field mouse dashes from out of the bucket, and from the sky a dark shadow swoops down and scoops up the field mouse. They build a small pile near Bull Cookies. The lights of the farm house are brighter, Highway #2 is silent, the pile has grown, and Bull Cookies has disappeared.

"There we go, Skin. Get ready-hey. This is going to be a big fire. It'll singe your hairs and you'll really be an Indian like me." Skiddo takes out a book of matches from his shirt pocket. He gets closer to some paper and small twigs, and he strikes the match. The sulphur makes him cough and the flame from the match dies out.

"Hurry up Skiddo-hey, I'm freezing."

Skiddo's second try is successful. The flame brings life to the paper, to the twigs, and to a piece of cloth.

"Hey." Skin moves closer to the fire.

"What?" Skiddo slowly straightens his body and shrugs to bring life into his back muscles.

"Where's Uncle?"

"He must've gone home. You know how old people are. Why are you worried about it?"

"I didn't see him leave."

"Shit Skin. He probably got mad and left."

"Yeah."

"I bet he's home right now and passed out by the stove."

"Uh-huh."

"At least we'll be warm and we have the bottle." Skiddo takes the bottle out from his pocket and takes a drink. He gives the bottle to Skin.

"Yeah, but I didn't see him leave at all."

ANDREA LERNER

Andrea Lerner is a writer and editor who considers western Oregon her "first home." She received her B.A. in American Studies from Reed College, Portland, Oregon, and her M.A. in Creative Writing from Stanford University. She has taught English at a number of schools including San Jose State University, California, Menlo College, Atherton, California, and Oregon State University in Corvallis. She is completing doctoral work in Comparative American Literatures at the University of Arizona. She makes her home in the foothills of the Tucson Mountains. She shares the yard with birds, lizards, and her dog Shoshone, and finds time "to watch the wind blow rivers of light across the mountains."

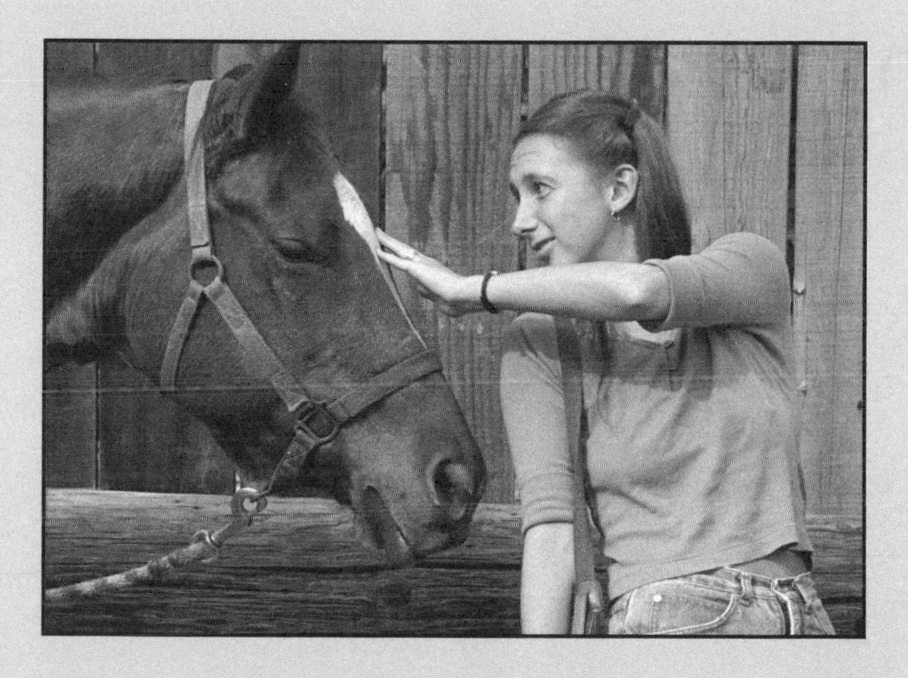

Bibliography

1. Books by Contributors

Barnes, James. *The La Plata Cantata*. West Lafayette, Indiana: Purdue University Press, 1988.

———. *A Season of Loss*. West Lafayette, Indiana: Purdue University Press, 1985.

———. *The American Book of the Dead*. Champaign: University of Illinois Press, 1982.

———. *The Fish on Poteau Mountain*, Cedar Creek Press, 1980.

———. *This Crazy Land*. Tempe, Arizona: Inland Boat Series, 1980.

Barnes, James, trans. *Summons And Sign: Poems by Dagmar Nick*. Translated from the German. Kirksville, Missouri: The Chariton Review Press, 1980.

Cardiff, Gladys. *To Frighten A Storm*. Port Townsend, Washington: Copper Canyon Press, 1976.

Chrystos. *Not Vanishing*. Vancouver, British Columbia: Press Gang, 1988.

Davis, Robert. *Soulcatcher*. Raven's Bones Press, 1986.

Endrezze, Anita. *Burning the Fields*. Confluence Press, 1983.

———. *The North Country*. Marvin, South Dakota: Blue Cloud Quarterly Press, 1983.

George, Phil. *Kautsas*. [Grandmothers] Nez Perce Tribe. Spaulding, Idaho, 1978.

Hale, Janet Campbell. *The Jailing of Cecilia Capture*. New York: Random House, 1985.

———. *Custer Lives in Humboldt County*. Greenfield Center, New York: Greenfield Review Press, 1977.

———. *The Owl's Song*. New York: Doubleday, 1974.

Niatum, Duane. *Drawings of the Song Animals: New and Selected Poems*. Duluth, Minnesota: Holy Cow Press, 1990.

———. *Stories of the Moons*. Marvin, South Dakota: Blue Cloud Quarterly Press, 1987.

———. *Songs for the Harvester of Dreams*. Seattle: University of Washington Press, 1981.

———. *Digging Out the Roots*. New York: Harper and Row, 1977.
———. *Ascending Red Cedar Moon*. New York: Harper and Row, 1974.
———. *After the Death of An Elder Klallam*. Phoenix: Baleen Press, 1970.
Northsun, Nila. *Diet Pepsi and Nacho Cheese*. Fallon, Nevada: Duck Down, 1977.
Salisbury, Ralph. *Going to the Water: Poems of a Cherokee Heritage*. Eugene, Oregon: Pacific House, 1983.
Sears, Vickie. *Simple Songs*. Ithaca, New York: Firebrand Books, 1990.
Swanson, R. A. *Breaking Stereotypes*. Poland: Weilichowo, 1986.
———. *Drummers, Dancers, and Singers*. [An Audio tape.] Pipestone, Minnesota: Featherstone Productions, 1986.
TallMountain, Mary. *Continuum*. Marvin, South Dakota: Blue Cloud Quarterly Press, 1988.
———. *There is No Word for Goodbye*. Marvin, South Dakota: Blue Cloud Quarterly Press, 1981.
Thompson, Earle. *The Juniper Moon Pulls At My Bones*. Marvin, South Dakota: Blue Cloud Quarterly Press, 1985.
Tremblay, Gail. *Indian Singing in Twentieth Century America*. Corvallis,Oregon: Calyx, 1989.
———. *Talking to the Grandfathers*. Omaha, Nebraska: Annex 21, #3 from The University of Nebraska.
Welch, James. *Fool's Crow*. New York: Harper and Row, 1987.
———. *The Death of Jim Loney*. New York: Harper and Row, 1979.
———. *Winter In the Blood*. New York: Harper and Row, 1974.
———. *Riding the Earthboy 40*. Rev. ed. New York: Harper and Row, 1975.
Whited, David. *The Fire's Purpose*. Burnaby, British Columbia: Cowan & Tetley, 1987.
Woody, Elizabeth. *Hand Into Stone*. New York: Contact II Press, 1988.

II. Anthologies of Contemporary American Indian Writing

Allen, Terry, ed. *The Whispering Wind: Poetry by Young American Indians*. Garden City, New Jersey: Doubleday, 1972.
Brandt, Beth. *A Gathering of Spirit*. Rockland, Maine: Sinister Wisdom Books, 1984.

Bruchac, Joseph, ed. *Songs From This Earth on Turtle's Back*. Greenfield Center, New York: Greenfield Review Press, 1983.

———. *Survival This Way: Interviews with American Indian Poets*. Tucson: University of Arizona Press, 1987.

Cochran, Jo, J. T. Stewart, and Mayumi Tsutakawa, ed. *Bearing Witness/Sobreviviendo: An Anthology of Native American/Latina Art and Literature*. Special issue of *Calyx: A Journal of Art and Literature by Women* 8 (2:Spring 1984). Corvallis, Oregon.

———. *Gathering Ground: New Writing and Art by Northwest Women of Color*. Seattle: Seal Press, 1984.

Conlon, Faith, *The Things That Divide Us: Stories by Women*. Seattle: Seal Press, 1985.

Dodge, Robert, ed. *Voices from Wah'kon'tah*. New York: International Publishers, 1974.

Green, Rayna, ed. *That's What She Said: Contemporary Poetry and Fiction By Native American Women*. Bloomington: Indiana University Press, 1984.

Hobson, Geary, ed. *The Remembered Earth*. Albuquerque: University of New Mexico Press, 1979.

Niatum, Duane, ed. *Harper's Anthology of 20th Century Native American Poetry*. San Francisco, California: Harper and Row, 1988.

———. *Carriers of the Dreamwheel*. New York: Harper and Row, 1975.

Ortiz, Simon. *Earth Power Coming*. Tsaile, Navajo Nation, Arizona: Navajo Community College Press, 1984.

Rosen, Kenneth, ed. *Voices of the Rainbow: Contemporary Poetry by American Indians*. New York: Viking Press, 1975.

———. *The Man to Send Rain Clouds: Contemporary Stories by American Indians*. New York: Viking, 1974.

III. Journals That Often Feature the Work of Northwest Native American Writers

Calapooya Collage. Edited by Thomas Ferte. P.O. Box 309, Monmouth, Oregon 97361.

Calyx: A Journal of Art and Literature by Women. Edited by Marguerite Donnally. P.O. Box B, Corvallis, Oregon 97339.

Journal of the Alaska Native Arts. P.O. Box 80583, Fairbanks, AK 99708.

Sinister Wisdom. Edited by Beth Brandt. Rockland, Maine.
Wicazo Sa Review. Edited by Elizabeth Cook Lynn. Eastern Washington State University, Cheney, Washington.

IV. Books on Traditional American Indian Literature of the Northwest

The following list is not meant to be a comprehensive bibliography but to point interested readers to major scholarship in the field and to acknowledge the connections between traditional and contemporary writing by Native Americans.

Boas, Franz. *Kwakiutl Tales*. New York: AMS, 1969.
Clark, Ella. *Indian Legends of the Pacific Northwest*. Berkeley: University of California Press, 1953.
Hilbert, Vi. *Haboo: Native American Stories from Puget Sound*. Seattle: University of Washington Press, 1985.
Hymes, Dell. *In Vain I Tried to Tell You: Essays in Native American Ethnopoetics*. Philadelphia: University of Pennsylvania Press, 1981.
Jacobs, Melville. *The Content and Style of an Oral Literature: Clackamas Chinook Myths and Tales*. Chicago: University of Chicago Press, 1959.
Jacobs, Melville, ed. *Clackamas Chinook Texts*. 2 vols. Bloomington: Indiana University Press, 1958 and 1959.
Kroeber, Karl, ed. *Traditional American Literature: Texts and Interpretations*. Lincoln: University of Nebraska Press, 1981.
Nelson, Richard K. *Make Prayers to the Raven: A Koyukon View of the Northern Forest*. Chicago: University of Chicago Press, 1983.
Phinney, Archie. *Nez Perce Texts*. (1934 reprint). New York: AMS, 1969.
Ramsey, Jarold. *Reading the Fire: Essays in the Traditional Indian Literature of the Far West*. Lincoln: University of Nebraska, 1983.
———. *Coyote Was Going There: Indian Literature of the Oregon Country*. Seattle: University of Washington Press, 1977.
Slickpoo, Allen, Sr., ed. *Nu-Mee-Poom Tit-Wah-Tit: Nez Perce Tales*. P. O. Box 305, Lapwai, Idaho: Nez Perce Tribe, 1972.
Swanton, John. *Tlingit Myths and Texts*. Bureau of American Ethnology Bulletin 39 (1909).

Barnes, Jim. "Near Crater Lake" and "At the Burn on the Oregon Coast" were published in Barnes, *A Season of Loss* (West Lafayette, Indiana: Purdue University Press, 1985). "One for Grand Ronde, Oregon" and "Contemporary Native American Poetry" appeared in Barnes, *American Book of the Dead* (Champaign: University of Illinois Press, 1982).

Chrystos. "I have not signed a treaty with the U.S. Government," "Dear Mr.President," "Winter Evening," "Over the top I go," and "Meditation for Gloria Anzaldua" all appeared in Chrystos, *Not Vanishing* (Vancouver, British Columbia: Press Gang, 1988).

Cochran, Jo Whitehorse. "Half-Breed Girl in City School" appeared in *Backbone: A Journal of Women's Literature*, Fall 1984.

Davis, Robert. "Soulcatcher," "Into the Forest," and "Drowning" all were published in Davis, *Soulcatcher* (Sitka, Alaska: Raven's Bones Press, 1986). "Into the Forest" and "Leveling Grave Island" have also been included in the forthcoming *Alaska State Arts Council Anthology* (Fairbanks: Alaska State Arts Council).

Endrezze, Anita. "October Morning Walk" appeared in Endrezze, *The North People* (Marvin, South Dakota: Blue Cloud Quarterly Press, vol. 29, no. 3, 1983).

Hale, Janet Campbell. "Autobiography in Fiction" originally appeared in *Jeopardy*, Spring 1987.

McGlashan, June. "Seagull Egg Story" appeared in the *Journal of Alaska Native Arts* (Fairbanks: Institute of Alaska Native Arts), May-June 1987.

Niatum, Duane. "Round Dance" appeared in *Wicazo Sa Review*, vol. 2, no. 1, Spring 1986. "Question of the Cedars" appeared in Niatum, *Song for the Harvester of Dreams* (Seattle: University of Washington Press, 1981). An unrevised version of "Old Tillicum" appeared in Niatum, *After the Death of an Elder Klallam* (Baleen Press 1970); "Son, This what I can tell you" appeared in *Chelsea Magazine* 47 (1988): 152–153.

Pratt, Agnes. "Empathy," "Death Takes Only A Minute," "So Quickly Came the Summer," and "Sympathy" first appeared in T. D. Allen, ed., *The Whispering Wind* (New York: Doubleday, 1972).

Simpson, Glen. "Front Street" first appeared in *Alaska Quarterly Review*, vol. 4, nos. 3–4 (1986); "Stick Dance, Nulato" appeared in *IANA Journal* (November–December 1986).

Swanson, Robert. "The Wanderer's Prayer" and "When the Spirit Moves You" appeared in *Iamiac Stereotypy (Breaking Stereotypes)*, Weilichowa, Poland, 1986. Both poems also were included in *Solemn Spirits* (Sweet Pine Press, 1974).

TallMountain, Mary. "Koyukons Heading Home" appeared in *A Press* (Laguna, New Mexico, 1978). "Drumbeats Somewhere Passing" was published in *Talking Leaf News* (Los Angeles, California, September 1982).

Thompson, Earle. "She Walks In New-Born Leaves" and "Vigil" appeared in Thompson, *The Juniper Moon Pulls At My Bones* (Marvin, South Dakota: Blue Cloud Quarterly Press, vol. 32, no. 2). "Afternoon Vigil" appeared in *Wicazo Sa Review*, vol. 3, no. 1, Spring 1987. "Whale Song" appeared in *Akewon*, no. 5, April 1986. "Spirit" was published in the *Yakima Nation Review*, vol. 19, no. 5, August 28, 1987. "Dancer" appeared in *Akewon*, December 1985.

Tremblay, Gail. "Coyote, Hanging In A Museum, Comes Off the Wall" appeared in *Native Visions*, a newsletter of the American Indian Contemporary Art, San Francisco, California. All of the poems in this volume are included in *Indian Singing in North America* (Corvallis, Oregon: Calyx, 1989).

Welch, James. "Riding the Earthboy 40," "Christmas Comes to Moccasin Flat," "The Only Bar in Dixon," and "Thanksgiving at Snake Butte" all appeared in Welch, *Riding the Earthboy 40* (New York: Harper & Row, revised edition, 1976).

Woody, Elizabeth. "Of Steps to Drowning," "Originating Fire," "Hand Into Stone," and "In Memory of Crossing the Columbia" appeared in Woody, *Hand Into Stone* (New York: Contact II Press, 1988).

Yellow Robe, William. "The Burning of Uncle" was published in *Journal of Ethnic Studies*, vol. 14, p. 3, Winter 1986, Pullman: Washington State University. It also appeared in *Cutbank*, vol. 24, Spring/Summer 1985 (Missoula: University of Montana English Department).

Portrait Credits

Gloria Bird, by Elizabeth Woody
Jim Barnes, by Ray Jagger
Chrystos, by Ana R. Kissed
Janet Campbell Hale, by Alice E. Bergeron
Andrea Lerner, by Gene Warneke
Dian Million, by Elizabeth Woody
Duane Niatum, by Mary Randlett
Ralph Salisbury, by E. M. Salisbury
Glen Simpson, by James H. Barker
Vickie Sears, by Linda Luster
Mary TallMountain, by Ullrich Zuckerman
Vince Wannassay, by Elizabeth Woody
James Welch, by Philip Red Eagle
Ramona Wilson, by Susan Lobo
Elizabeth Woody, by Jaqueline Moreau